THREE TOURS THROUGH LONDON

London, *c.* 1748. Somerset House Gardens are in the Foreground

THREE TOURS *THROUGH* LONDON *IN THE YEARS* 1748—1776—1797

By Wilmarth Sheldon Lewis

GREENWOOD PRESS, PUBLISHERS
WESTPORT, CONNECTICUT

Originally published in 1941 as Vol. 21 (1941) of
The Colver Lectures, Brown University, by
Yale University Press

Reprinted with the permission of
Yale University Press

First Greenwood Reprinting 1971

Library of Congress Catalogue Card Number 77-104252

SBN 8371-3977-5

Printed in the United States of America

TO

ANNIE BURR LEWIS

CONTENTS

LIST OF ILLUSTRATIONS

The maps at end are from John Roque, *Plan of London*, 1746.

PREFACE

THE questions I have set out to answer here are these: If we could be transported to London in the years 1748, 1776, 1797, what would we find? How did the people live? What were they like? What would we see and do? What would be the *feel* of the place? Oddly enough, no one seems to have tried to do this for specific years;[1] there are books on every conceivable aspect of eighteenth-century life, but they cover the entire century.

No two tourists, in any age or place, choose the same things to see or do. I am more interested in the theatre, for example, than in the Royal Exchange; consequently, there is quite a lot about the theatre in these tours and nothing about the Royal Exchange. Again, if instead of being preoccupied with Horace Walpole, I were preoccupied with Hume, let us say, or with Burke or John Wesley, these tours would have been quite different; but to repeat a remark on page 5, tourists are not expected to see everything.

These 'tours' were first given as lectures at Brown University in the spring of 1941. I have been unable to resist stuffing in new bits here and there, but I have

1. I discovered after I had started writing these lectures that Sir Walter Besant has a delightful passage in his *London in the Eighteenth Century*, 1902, pp. 133–9, which does for 1716 what I have attempted to do for 1748, 1776, 1797. His sole source was Gay's *Trivia*.

forced myself to stop doing so, because there is no limit to what might be added.

I hope those readers who dislike footnotes will forgive me for making so many: a book of this character is rubbish without them. I hope, too, that they will not mind having them at the foot of the page where they belong. Nothing, I think, is more irritating than the practice of hiding the notes at the back of the book so as not to distract the attention of readers of delicate concentration. Nothing is better reading (except a good index) than footnotes, and it is monstrous to keep them out of sight as if they were poor or idiotic relations whose existence must be kept from the knowledge of callers in the parlour.

My indebtedness to published work is indicated in the notes and in the bibliography at the end of the book. Here I wish to thank the following who have answered queries or made helpful suggestions: Messrs Curtis Bradford, John F. Fulton, Edgar S. Furniss, Miles L. Hanley, Allen T. Hazen, Bernhard Knollenberg, George L. Lam, Hermann Liebert, John Hill Morgan, Allardyce Nicoll, the Rev. T. L. Riggs, Warren Hunting Smith (who also read the proofs), James T. Soby, Chauncey Brewster Tinker, Ralph M. Williams, Miss Mary Alden Hopkins, and Miss Julia McCarthy. I am indebted to Mrs Richard G. Gettell for making the index. My wife not only read many books for me, but was of the greatest possible help in the selection and arrangement of the material finally used.

W. S. L.

Farmington, May 1941.

A TOUR THROUGH LONDON
1748

1748

FIRST of all, I should explain that I have chosen the years of our tours arbitrarily in the half of the eighteenth century which is most familiar to me. Professors of English literature tell us that the eighteenth century properly ends in 1798, with the publication of *The Lyrical Ballads*. Since I want to cover half a century, the years of our first and last tours are automatically fixed, and there can be no hesitation for a patriotic American in choosing a year between. It is 1776, of course.

Our character of tourists is a convenient one for many reasons, but for none more so than for the indulgence which is extended to tourists, even when they give lectures about their tours. That there should be this indulgence is odd since everybody knows that such travellers are notoriously superficial and inaccurate. The judgments arrived at on a visit of a few weeks, even though one may have dined nightly with the wisest and the most beautiful in the land, are laughable in the opinion of the natives and contemptible in the opinion of the truly informed. But indulgence there is, perhaps because if the tourist shows little else, he does show interest in his subject, and that is ingratiating, no matter how inept he may be.

If the tourist's remarks about his contemporaries are inadequate, how much more inadequate must they be about a society which lived two hundred years before his time? It is true that when we talk about the distant past we have certain advantages which are lacking when we talk about the present: we have the advantage of perspective and the knowledge of the causes of events and the factors in decisions which led to them. We can see our chosen period in relation to what went before it and to what followed after it; but there our advantages end.

Who has not had the experience of returning to a place where he once lived and finding it changed?

> *Glion?—Ah, twenty years, it cuts*
> *All meaning from a name!*
> *White houses prank where once were huts.*
> *Glion, but not the same!*

Even when the change is subtle, when perhaps the house you lived in and the houses about it still stand, even if your family or friends still live in them, everything is different. The mere passing of the years has changed them; it has changed you, too, and the houses and the gardens, and the streets. For you and your family and friends the past is a chapter now closed, except for your imperfect recollections of it. An accident may remind you of a long-forgotten moment—the reading of a letter you wrote when a child, the smell of poplars in the summer heat, some such thing—

you are arrested and startled, but in the next moment the book which is your past is closed again and the page you have just seen is buried within it.

This change, this refraction, goes on about us all the time. From having been aware of only two generations we become aware of a third, a younger one, as strange to us as the older one, for it has no memory of the world we grew up in and it sees the present with its own eyes. Anyone over forty can remember when no lady worthy of the name went into the sea without benefit of black stockings, when cigarettes were a sign of decadence even in men, and when the automobile was a symbol of revolt from the ways of decent horse-drawn people. Such a world is as strange to those born after 1920 as the world of Lincoln or of Pericles.

Since we have difficulty in understanding the generations nearest to us, how can we have the temerity to discuss a period which is six or seven generations removed? The hardihood of attempting tours in the eighteenth century is undeniably great, but if we recognize at the outset the limitations of our project, and if we stick resolutely to what facts we can assemble, we may not do too badly; and, in retrospect, we can excuse our temerity by remembering that, however diligent and eager tourists may be, they are not, after all, expected to see everything.

The transition to the eighteenth century presents a problem. In the play *Berkeley Square*, you remember, the hero parted the curtains up stage and cried, 'Berkeley Square! I thought it would be like this.' That proves him to have been a very great scholar indeed. Unhappily, I cannot speak to you with his certitude.

Nor can I put before you prints of eighteenth-century life and photographs of its pictures and turn a crank and have them stir and move into life. This would of course be the most scholarly solution of the problem. The ladies and gentlemen in the pictures of Zoffany and Devis would rise from their chairs with a rustle of silk and bow and curtsy; the unfortunate women at Bridewell would pound their hemp; the naked wretch at Bedlam would pull at his chains and shriek at the idiot fiddling outside his cell; and the upraised club would crack upon the head of the dog. This uninvented time-machine would give you the sights and sounds of eighteenth-century London. There would be nothing left for me to do but to convey to you its smell.

In the absence of such a machine we can only proceed with the help of maps and newspapers, of prints, and letters and journals, particularly those written by tourists who, like ourselves, were visiting eighteenth-century London for the first time.

Let's start off boldly then, in 1748. It is early in May. We have landed at Dover where we have found the customs officers to be as formidable as their twentieth-century descendants, and we have taken a post chaise and pair for London, for which we pay at the twentieth-century rate of a shilling a mile.[1] (We are going to do ourselves well on these tours; we might have come in a stagecoach for a fifth the sum.[2]) As it is, although we have broken the trip by spending a night at Rochester on the way, our carriage has no springs and we have been racked by the road. For the last few miles as we crossed the Surrey fields we have been sustained by the familiar sight of St Paul's and at this precise moment we are entering the borough of Southwark, which with the cities of Westminster and London composes the metropolis. Southwark is 'a quarter of the town ill-built, having but two streets in its breadth, and almost entirely occupied by tanners and weavers.'[3]

In this overwhelming moment of arrival, amid a thousand unfamiliar details of buildings, streets, and people, what strikes us first? We have been prepared for the fancy-dress aspect of London, although, unless we are students of costume, we have probably not pictured the current mode, the wide, flat hoops and straw hats of the women; the long coats and waistcoats of the men; and the children dressed the same as their elders; for when we have thought of eighteenth-century dress we have usually pictured that of the 'seventies and

1. *Travels of Carl Philipp Moritz in England in* 1782, edn 1926, p. 18.
2. W[illiam] T. Jackman, *The Development of Transportation in Modern England*, Cambridge, 1916, ii. 703.
3. P. J. Grosley, *A Tour to London*, trans. Thomas Nugent, 1772, i. 24.

'eighties. There are of course no fine clothes in Southwark, and, in spite of our diligence in poring over Hogarth, we are horrified by the rags and filth and by the deformed and twisted bodies and the noses eaten away by disease. A shiver of fear runs down our spines, since the Watch is a poor substitute for the friendly bobbies of the twentieth century, and although these people are about half a foot shorter than the average height of 1941,[3a] their very smallness increases in us the sense of seeing sub-human beings from another and more evil planet. We pay, at this first encounter, little attention to the tumble-down buildings at this end of the town, but they contribute to the nightmare. Our eyes are on the dreadful, unpaved road. There are no gutters, but a narrow ditch runs through the middle of the floundering street into which filth of every description, offal, dead cats and dogs, and night soil, is heaped. There are no sidewalks here, but footways are marked off from the road by posts placed at intervals. The hooves of our horses and the wheels of our carriage fling the muck to right and left and we now understand the advantage of the wall and why gentlemen even in the twentieth century walk between the street and their ladies. But there is no question what is the strongest impression, and we have instinctively followed eighteenth-century practice and put up

3a. This is a guess. The Yale University Department of Health, Section of Physical Education, 16 Nov. 1939, shows that the average height of the Yale Freshman Class of 1943 was 69.97 inches, 2.37 inches taller than the Freshman Class of 1893.

the glasses of our carriage. We have done so partly to protect ourselves from the wash of passing vehicles, but there is a second reason: we feel that the eighteenth-century German traveller was tongue-tied when he referred to the 'insupportable stench.'[4] This one of our squeamish twentieth-century apprehensions of eighteenth-century London has been immediately confirmed.

We are in one of the many sections of London which might have sat for Hogarth's 'Gin Lane.'[5] This is the period when the ravages of gin have reached such an extent that at last the public conscience is slowly moving to their abatement. Its use had been encouraged at the beginning of the century by Parliament 'as one of the most essential things to support the landed interest that any branch of trade can help us to.'[6] Never, it is probably safe to say, have human beings sunk to such depths as have the London poor in 1748. 'Drunk for a penny, dead drunk for two-pence, clean straw for nothing,'[7] is literally true, except for the clean straw. 'Gin [wrote Henry Fielding in 1751, when he had had two years' experience as a magistrate] . . . is the principal sustenance (if it may be so called) of more than an hundred thousand people in this metropolis. Many of these wretches there are, who swallow pints of this poison within the twenty-four hours; the dreadful

4. Moritz, p. 227.
5. Published in 1751. Its actual site in Hogarth's picture was St Giles.
6. Daniel Defoe, *Review*, 9 May 1713.
7. The sign on a dram shop in 'Gin Lane.'

effects of which I have the misfortune every day to see, and to smell, too.'[8] 'More than an hundred thousand people' is approximately a fifth of the entire population of London. Crimes of violence are of course common, and it is not remarkable that at this time infant mortality in certain East End parishes has reached one hundred per cent. Gin-ridden mothers expose their babies in the streets; the children that survive, a contemporary report states, 'starved and naked at home . . . either become a burthen to their parishes or . . . are forced to beg whilst they are children, and as they grow up learn to pilfer and steal.'[9] Their histories are told by Hogarth in 'The Idle Apprentice' and 'The Harlot's Progress.'

Nothing can induce us, unless we are professional social workers, to return to so appalling a section of London, not even the sight of the ships of all nations crowded in the River for miles below London Bridge, which is now before us, loading and unloading their cargoes in mid-stream by lighters and barges and bringing to England that wealth which is presently to make her the greatest nation in the world. We are content to accept that forest of masts as an unequalled marvel of eighteenth-century Europe, along with Billingsgate, Wapping, Limehouse, and Poplar, the ham-

8. Henry Fielding, *An Enquiry into the Causes of the late Increase of Robbers*, *Works*, 1751, p. 18, quoted by Miss M. Dorothy George in *Johnson's England*, ed. A. S. Turberville, Oxford, 1933, i. 312.

9. *Order Book*, Middlesex Sessions, Jan. 1735–6, quoted bv Miss M. Dorothy George, *London Life*, 1925, p. 34.

lets and parishes which cater to the shore requirements of the sailors and which also hold world's records of their own.

Now we pass through the stone gateway on the Southwark side of London Bridge, the only completed bridge across the Thames in 1748. There are brick houses on the bridge which rise to three stories and hang crazily out over the water. This is one of the unforgettable pictures of our tours- The roadway on the bridge between the houses is just wide enough for two coaches to pass,[10] but the foot passengers must look out for themselves. We move along on the left[11] and catch glimpses of shops on either side. 'I well remember,' writes Thomas Pennant, 'the street on London Bridge, narrow, darksome, and dangerous to passengers from the multitude of carriages: frequent arches of strong timber crossed the street, from the tops of the houses, to keep them together, and from falling into the river. Nothing but use could preserve the rest of the inmates, who soon grew deaf to the noise of the falling waters, the clamours of watermen, or the frequent shrieks of drowning wretches.'[12] These last were not only suicides but watermen and their passengers overturned in the waters that rush under the arches of the bridge. In the middle of the bridge we come to an open space, London Square, from which on one side we

10. Gordon Home, *Old London Bridge*, 1931, p. 260.
11. Ibid. 258.
12. Ibid. 254, quoting Thomas Pennant, *Of London*, 1790, pp. 296–7.

see the Tower and the thousands of masts at a nearer view and on the other side we look up the River to the Abbey with the spires of Wren's churches and the tower of York Buildings Water Works forming the sky-line between. The garden of Somerset House breaks the line of the buildings. On the River itself there is a busy to-ing and fro-ing of innumerable small craft: sail boats, the ten-to-eighteen-oared barges of the great, and small rowboats carrying passengers along what is still a London thoroughfare. The colour and animation of the River are delightful. The watermen wear red or blue breeches and white coats and often they have red or black caps of velvet or cloth; the seats of the rowboats are bright red or green.[13] All along the banks are 'stairs' which serve as stations; beside them are tall, slender poles for the boats to tie to, like the poles in Venice. Boys are swimming and splashing about the stairs.

We continue on the bridge through sixteenth-century Nonsuch House and presently pass St Magnus Martyr and the Monument. We are now in the City of London, the commercial and financial centre of England, and from this point onwards we catch glimpses of the familiar among the strange. We proceed along Fish Street Hill and Lombard Street to the Mansion House, which we welcome as an old friend of the twentieth century.

13. César de Saussure, *A Foreign View of England in the Reigns of George I and George II*, 1902, p. 169. The colours may be seen in the pictures of Samuel Scott.

It is all much cleaner and wholesomer than Southwark and the buildings rise to four and five stories. Cornhill comes in as we remember it, but a block of buildings shuts off our view of the Royal Exchange and the Bank. There is of course no Queen Victoria Street and we go westward through the Poultry and Cheapside to St Paul's. Circling St Paul's we go down Ludgate Hill and over Fleet Bridge. On our left is the appalling Fleet River, here called Fleet Ditch, which is virtually an open sewer gliding into the Thames.

Eighteenth-century London is an enormous ant palace with myriads of courts and yards and alleys that twist off through narrowing and widening lanes into rectangular pockets which, as often as not, have no further outlet. 'The confused babel,' we are to read in the newspaper, *Old England*, on the 2d of July 1748, 'the confused *Babel* which now appears to us, with the *Hotch-Potch* of half-moon and serpentine narrow Streets, close, dismal, long Lanes, stinking Allies, dark, gloomy Courts and suffocating Yards, etc.' There was, the writer admits, an occasional fine structure, such as a church or hospital, but the builders were careful 'to thrust it, as it were, into some Hole out of Sight, or erect some smoaky Shed against it, so as to cover it from Observation, as if they were ashamed of having laid out their Money in so *useless* a Manner, and so unconducive to Trade and Business . . . If we look into the Streets,' he continues, 'what a Medley of Neighbourhood do we see? Here lives a Personage of high Distinction; next Door a Butcher with his stinking Shambles! A Tallow-Chandler shall front my Lord's nice *Venetian* Window; and two or three brawny naked Curriers [leather-dressers] in their Pits shall face a fine Lady in her back Closet, and disturb her spiritual Thoughts: At one End of the Street shall be a Chandler's Shop to debauch all the neighbouring Maids with Gin and gossipping Tales, and at the other End perhaps a Brasier, who shall thump out a noisy Disturbance, by a Ring of Hammerers, for a Quarter of a Mile round him. In the Vicinity of some good Bishop, some good *Mother* frequently hangs out her Flag. The Riotous, from their filthy Accommodations of a *Spring Garden* Bagnio, shall echo their *Bacchanalian* Noise to the Devotions of the *opposite* Chapel, which may perhaps *sue in vain for a Remedy to any* BOARD. Thus we go on in *England*, and all this owing wholly to private Interest and Caprice.'

Fleet Ditch made us close our windows, and at Temple Bar we receive another shock, for fixed upon it are three rotting human heads. They originally belonged to rebels of the '45, and they are to stay on Temple Bar until they fall down, one by one, many years hence. This shock is of another and profounder kind, for it opens an abyss between the eighteenth-century mind and ours. The eighteenth century looks upon these heads and the bodies of highwaymen hanging in chains along the highways as wholesome examples of what happens to you when you commit treason or rob a coach. Their heads and their bodies are acquired with all possible publicity: 'Sir,' says Dr Johnson, 'executions are intended to draw spectators. If they do not draw spectators, they do not answer their purpose,' and he deplores the doing away of public executions; 'The public was gratified by a procession, the criminal was supported by it.'[14] The eighteenth century is more honest, as well as more robust, about punishment than are we of the twentieth century, who require that the third degree and the concentration camp be kept out of sight. During our tour we may at any time come upon a man standing in the pillory being pelted by mud and filth, or see persons flogged through the streets, and even while strolling in the Mall, the most fashionable walk in London, we may, if we choose, witness the application of a thousand lashes (literally) to the naked back of a single soldier.

It is clear, even in the short space of our passage from Southwark to the Strand, that something is wrong with the Art Shoppe view of eighteenth-century London, the beaux and belles of old London type of thing, which shows Milady being gracefully handed out of her sedan chair by Milord and both dressed up to the nines. Because the eighteenth century is a popular period at fancy dress parties we instinctively romanticize it. Now

14. James Boswell, *Life*, ed. Hill and Powell, iv. 188.

as we pass along the Strand, we can let down our windows and be delighted with the sight and sound of the London we had pictured. There *are* sedan chairs swaying gently along between the two chairmen and there may be a gentleman inside instead of a lady. There are street-cries, 'Chairs to Mend!' 'Scissors to grind!' 'Remember the poor debtors!' and bunches of lavender and dolls and printed ballads pushed into our windows, along with the stumps the ubiquitous beggars thrust upon us to excite our charity. The bells of London are a surprise, not the church bells with their enthusiastic bell-ringers, but the individual bells of the dustmen, the sweeps, knife-grinders, old clothesmen, and postmen.

The tradesmen's signs we have been prepared for are hanging before the shops which we shall find one of the inexhaustible delights of our tours. Many of the signs are exceedingly well-done—Hogarth himself painted some—and we never tire of their heraldry: 'The Dolphin and Comb,' 'The Lamb and Inkbottle,' and a vast company of monsters, fishes, and martyrs. In the absence of numbers these signs are the street addresses of their owners and eighteenth-century Londoners memorize their locations. Their tradesmen's cards and invoices read like this:

'Millis & ffossick [Wire-drawers] At the Black Horse, over against the Church in Crooked-Lane.'

'Ann Badger [wine & spirit merchant], At the

China Jar, in Cannon Street, near Grace-church Street.'[15]

That is to say, one flounders about when finding a new address. Like so many of London's picturesque features the signs have their inconvenient side, for they creak horribly in the wind and they not only drip dismally upon the passerby but they fall down without warning.

From the heart of the City onwards we have been passing these signs and their shops, which are unrivalled in Europe. They have, often, bow-front windows and a glass door, 'through which every article that is elegant and fashionable,' says a foreign visitor, 'may be seen, arranged with the utmost taste and symmetry. . . . Nothing can be more superb than the silver-smiths' shops. In looking at the prodigious quantity of plate piled up and exposed there, one can only form a proper idea of the riches of the nation. The greatest shops in St Honoré at Paris, appear contemptible when compared with those in London.'[16] The nation of shopkeepers takes its vocation seriously; shop-keeping is an art. In *The London Tradesman* for 1747 appear the qualifications for 'a gold and silver laceman: He ought to speak fluently, though not elegantly, to entertain the ladies: and to be master of a handsome bow and cringe: should be

15. From trade-cards and invoices kindly supplied by Sir Ambrose Heal from his great collection.

16. J. W. von Archenholz, *A Picture of England*, 1789, i. 151–2.

able to hand a lady to and from her coach politely, without being seized with a palpitation of the heart at the touch of a delicate hand, the sight of a well-turned and much exposed limb, or a handsome face.'[17]

We creep along in the jam of street traffic to Charing Cross, where Dr Johnson said was the full tide of human existence. It is very confusing without Trafalgar Square and with the only familiar landmark Charles I on his horse, but the names of the next streets are perfectly familiar: Cockspur Street, the Haymarket, Pall Mall, St James's Street, with St James's Palace at the bottom of it and Piccadilly roaring along at the top.

We have taken lodgings, the universal practice of visitors not staying with friends or relatives, for there are no hotels and the coaching inns are too noisy and of course too 'low.' We turn off St James's Street into Little Ryder Street, our carriage comes to a stop before the door of our landlady, Miss Ridley, the coachman gets down to help us out, the front door of our lodgings opens and the servants of the house hurry out to help with our luggage. We heave ourselves up from the seat on which we have suffered so much to step

17. R. Campbell, *The London Tradesman*, 1747, p. 147; quoted by George, *Johnson's England*, i. 176. *The General Shop Book: or, The Tradesman's Universal Director*, 1753, defines Laceman: 'The gold and silver Laceman deals in lace, fringes, embroidery, net-work, orrice, gold and silver-wire; buttons, spangles, purle and twist. He takes 100 l. usually with an apprentice. His journeymen are as great beaus [*sic*] as the mercer's; and have 70 or 80 pounds per ann. wages. It will require upwards of 1000 l. to set up a Laceman.'

into eighteenth-century London as Miss Ridley herself appears in the doorway and—at this point I must let you down very badly, for this is not the play *Berkeley Square* and I don't honestly know what comes next. What, for example, does our hostess sound like when she talks? Assuming (to make it easy) that Miss Ridley speaks the best English of her day, she probably sounds more like a Down East Yankee than anything else.[18] Certainly she does not utter the refined notes of the English twentieth century, and we have, at least at first, some trouble in understanding her. As for the cockney servants, their speech is all but impossible for us. But we must struggle on: Miss Ridley shows us to our rooms which consist of a bedroom and dressing room, for which we pay thirty shillings a week. This includes a room for our servant. We may have breakfast, dinner, and coffee if we choose, for a few shillings extra. Breakfast at this time of year consists of tea (with cream or sweet milk), bread and butter, and that is all, for the huge English breakfasts are a century in the future. The hour for breakfast is about ten.[19] Dinner is at about four in 1748 and is for many the last meal of the day. Those who do have supper have it at nine or ten and have only cold meat and cheese.[20] Tea has not yet become a separate meal, but floods of it are drunk during

18. I am indebted to Prof. Miles L. Hanley for this information.

19. Pehr Kalm, *Account of His Visit to England*, trans. Joseph Lucas, 1892, pp. 13 ff.

20. Ibid. p. 16.

the day and night by all classes in spite of, or possibly because of, the attack recently made on its use by the Methodists,[21] who are convinced of its wickedness. Coffee is served after dinner, several cups of it, and it is execrable.[21a]

Count Kielmansegge who is to take these rooms after us describes them as having the 'common mahogany furniture, which is found in most houses here.'[22] There are a table and two chairs and 'presses' for our clothes, in place of closets. There are sheets on the bed, as well as blankets, and underneath the bottom sheet is another blanket, a luxury unknown on the continent of Europe.[23] The eighteenth century does not share the nineteenth century's passion for a glut of furniture. Eighteenth-century rooms seem stark and uncomfortable, in spite of our admiration of their proportions, their ceilings, their over-mantels, their tables, and chairs. In 1748, those who cannot afford Mr Chippendale's and Mr Kent's new secretary-bookcases and pie-crust tables have to worry along with their Queen Anne walnut. Rooms which are so fortunate as to be papered with Mr Bromwich's new wallpapers have acquired a certain gaiety, but eighteenth-century rooms are not informal.

21. See John Wesley's *Journal*, 6 July 1746.

21a. See Barthélemy Faujas de Saint Fond, *A Journey through England and Scotland . . . in* 1784, Glasgow, 1907, i. 49, 57, 254.

22. Count Frederick Kielmansegge, *Diary of a Journey to England in the Years* 1761–1762, 1902, p. 20.

23. Carl Philipp Moritz, *Travels in England in* 1782, Oxford, 1926, p. 34.

The Thomlinson Family
From the painting by Arthur Devis, 1745

Piccadilly at St James's Street, 1750

We leave Miss Ridley's as soon as we can to walk about this part of London. Since we are dressed exactly in the English style of the moment, we are not liable to the indignities which, sooner or later, we should certainly receive if we were suspected of being foreigners. Furthermore, we are in exactly the right clothes for walking the streets in the day-time; if we were over-dressed 'the mob' would throw mud at us, even were we royalty itself. We thread our way between the carriages in Piccadilly, which are so numerous here that a man in a hurry abandons his carriage and walks. The lay of the land continues to be wonderfully familiar as we walk up Bond Street. There is a delightful change at Grafton Street, which is called Evans Row, for the end of the blocks formed by Albemarle and Dover Streets are gardens. Clifford Street, Bruton Street, Conduit, Grosvenor, Madox, and Brook Streets, all are unchanged. Hanover Square is the same, with Hanover Street and Princes Street running off into, not Regent Street, of course, but Great Swallow Street. We reach Oxford Street, here called Tyburn Road, and turn west. To the north are open fields and the hills of Hampstead and Highgate; we have reached London's frontier. Kensington, Hammersmith, and Kew are near-by villages. The houses end at North Audley Street, but we go on to Tyburn Lane, which is to become Park Lane. At the future site of the Marble Arch is the gallows of Tyburn itself and the corner where the twentieth-century orators are to harangue small, indifferent crowds is the place 'where soldiers are shot.'[24] We go down Tyburn Lane, Hyde Park on our right, and presently pass Chesterfield House, one of the finest houses in London. Lord Chesterfield and Tyburn are near neighbours. One can picture Chesterfield sitting at his writing desk instructing his illegitimate son in the one great essential of life: grace. 'Let the great book of the world be your serious study; read it over and over, get it by heart, adopt its style, and make it your own. . . . Endeavour to please others, and divert yourself as much as ever you can.'[25] While he wrote those words, or thousands of others like them, there may have come through the windows of Chesterfield House the shouts of the mob, which Dr Johnson approved, attending the condemned to Tyburn, or the sound of a volley of musketry. We are never far from these contrasts in the eighteenth century and they are as chilling to us as is the sudden sharp statement by a friend of a position unalterably opposed to our own.

We reach Hyde Park Corner, a dreary frontier strip of houses protected by a turnpike, and cross on down Constitution Hill through the Green Park to Buckingham House (not yet a Palace). Where Belgravia is to be in the next century are

24. John Roque, *Plan of London*, 1746, plate 2. It is used as a front endpaper of this book.

25. 9 July 1750 O.S.

open fields. St James's Park stretches before Buckingham House, a canal running through the middle of it and 'a stinking body of water,' Rosamond's Pond, on one side. On the north is the Mall, with its four rows of trees. We turn to the left between Marlborough House and St James's Palace, and are home again in a few minutes. Except for the small section in the neighbourhood of the Abbey and the Houses of Parliament, we have in this walk of a little over an hour traversed the bounds of the Court End of Town.

The foreigner in 1748 lost no time in seeing the sights. Four of these we of the twentieth century have also seen: The Tower (although in 1748 it has lions in its moat), the Royal Exchange, St Paul's, and the Abbey. Bedlam is one of the places where visitors always go. We may take tea, if we choose, with the milder inmates, to the accompaniment of the shrieks of others chained to their beds.[26] Instead of doing this we go to Ranelagh, in Chelsea, and to Vauxhall, which is across the River on the Surrey side. The eighteenth century cannot find words to describe them. Their gardens are unrivalled for the beauty of their walks and the brilliance of their lights. There is music, but no dancing. At Vauxhall supper is served in boxes built in the form of Chinese kiosques. At both gardens even the best company goes in 'undress'; in fact, Vauxhall, as a young Irishman says, 'is a

26. See Grosley, i. 242–4.

general place of rendezvous, where intrigues of all sorts are commonly carried on, and pity it is that so enchanting a place is so often made the instrument of so much wickedness.'[27]

One night in June 1748 Horace Walpole went to Vauxhall. 'As I was coming out,' he writes, 'I was overtaken by a great light, and retired under the trees of Marble Hall to see what it should be. There came a long procession of Prince Lobkowitz's footmen in very rich new liveries, the two last bearing torches; and after them the Prince himself, in a new sky-blue watered tabby coat, with gold buttonholes, and a magnificent gold waistcoat fringed, leading Madame l'Ambassadrice de Venise in a green sack with a straw hat, attended by my Lady Tyrawley,' and several others. 'They went into one of the Prince of Wales's barges, had another barge filled with violins and hautboys, and an open boat with drums and trumpets.'[28] This is the sort of thing we may stumble upon at any moment in the eighteenth century.

Ranelagh has no 'dark walks,' but it makes up in importance what it lacks in wickedness. Its great feature is the Rotunda, about one hundred and eighty feet in diameter. 'When I first entered Ranelagh,' said Dr Johnson, 'it gave an expansion and gay sensation to my mind, such as I never

27. Anon, *Narrative of the Journey of an Irish Gentleman through England in the Year* 1752, ed. W. C. Hazlitt 1869, p. 95.

28. Walpole to Conway, 27 June 1748.

The Rotunda at Ranelagh

experienced any where else.'[29] It is divided into three stories; the first contains boxes, each with a table and seats for ten persons; the second story also has boxes with movable lattices which assure privacy if privacy is wanted; and the third story is a gallery in which there are an organ and choir. An odd arrangement of fireplaces on pillars is in the middle of the huge room, at which are produced tea, coffee, and punch. There are tables all about, and around and around the room for years and years and years solemnly march the greatest and most fashionable figures of the eighteenth century in their orders and ribbons and dignity. It is no wonder foreigners stare; we stare on our visits. We never tire of Ranelagh, for every night we may see the men and women whose letters and diaries we have read, whose portraits by Hudson, Richardson, and, above all, by Hogarth, have already been painted and who are going to be painted by Ramsay, Reynolds, and Gainsborough. Ranelagh is enormously popular, and although it is no farther than Chelsea, our coach may be over an hour in getting there,[30] particularly in May, for May is the height of the season at the Gardens. After June the Great World leaves London a desert by going to their homes in the country, and Ranelagh and Vauxhall do not survive August.

29. Boswell, *Life*, iii. 199.

30. 'Disagreeable Ranelagh, which is so crowded, that going there t'other night in a string of coaches, we had a stop of six and thirty minutes.' (Walpole to Montagu, 26 May 1748.)

Ranelagh and Vauxhall are the chief reason why we commence our tours in May.

We lean over the gallery at Ranelagh and come to recognize the rulers of 1748 as we come to recognize, by frequent attendance, the players on a team: the Grenvilles, the Russells, and the Cavendishes; the Duke of Newcastle and his brother, Henry Pelham, Lady Caroline and Henry Fox, the future Lord Mansfield, Horace Walpole, the Princess Amelia and Lady Mary Coke. The men have been educated at Eton and Westminster, Oxford and Cambridge; the women have not been 'educated' at all. The men have made the Grand Tour and come back to find themselves sitting in Parliament for a family borough. The women have been given in marriage after prolonged negotiations between family lawyers and conveyancers and have gone to work to produce the children, so many of whom proceed immediately to the family graveyards. Around and around they all go before us to the measures of Handel and Corelli and Pergolesi.[31]

Seventeen hundred and forty-eight is a dull year politically. The Pelhams are poor things compared to their predecessor, Robert Walpole, and their successor, Lord Chatham. It is the year when the War of the Austrian Succession (better known to us, perhaps, as King George's War) fizzles out in the Peace of Aix-la-Chapelle. The account that

31. See Carl Philipp Moritz, *Travels in England in* 1782, 1926, pp. 46–50, for a delightful account of Ranelagh.

Spain had acceded to the preliminaries of peace arrived in London on the 20th of May, and the 'armed vessels in the service of his Majesty's navy were all ordered to be paid off and discharged.'[32] The Peace is to be signed on the 18th of October and it is to describe itself as 'a Christian, universal, and perpetual peace.'[33] All lands taken by either side are to be restored and there is never, never, never to be war again, but London is so self-contained about it that it is to wait six months to celebrate,[34] and, in the meantime, it is going right to work to prepare for the next war which is to come in eight years. Accounts of ships captured by both sides continue to appear in *The Gentleman's Magazine* for May, June, July, 1748, and among the 'ships taken by the English' are many whose captors are men of Rhode Island and Providence Plantations who carried their prizes into Newport and Providence. That is, we have a stake in the endless parade around the Rotunda. It joins us to India to form the first British Empire which we are presently to dismember.

The Parade realizes dimly that it has a stake in North America, a financial and commercial stake. The Colonies represent certain emoluments, too, in the way of sinecures, to be given away to

32. *The Gentleman's Magazine*, June 1748, xviii. 281.

33. Ibid., Nov. 1748, xviii. 493.

34. The Peace was celebrated by an elaborate display of fireworks, 25 April 1749, which were only partially successful, but did manage to burn down part of the pavilion erected for the celebration. See Walpole's animated account of it to Mann, 3 May 1749.

friends and relations; furthermore, America is a convenient place to transport criminals. The Parade's attitude towards America is not unlike our attitude towards the Philippines three or four decades ago: excellent to have under one's flag, no doubt, for all its being so remote, and many merchants and gentlemen are making money out of it. In that useful contemporary work, *The Present State of Great Britain*,[35] we find the Governors and Officers in the West Indies listed in this order: Jamaica, Barbadoes, Leeward Islands, Bahama Islands, Bermuda, South Carolina, North Carolina, Virginia, Pennsylvania, Maryland, New York, New Jersey, Georgia, Gibraltar, Minorca, Rhode Island and Providence Plantations, Connecticut, Massachusetts, New Hampshire, Nova Scotia, and Newfoundland, and we are reminded of the Duke of Newcastle's surprise when he discovered that Cape Breton was an island.

In time, as we gaze down upon the Parade, we come to discriminate niceties of dress and manner. The eighteenth century is far more ceremonious than the twentieth and more importance is attached to ease of movement. The dress of the men is susceptible of a thousand significances and because it is as individualistic and as expensive as the dress of the women it constitutes a study in itself: the choice of materials and colours, the style

35. John Chamberlayne, *Magnae Britanniæ Notitia: or, The Present State of Great Britain*, 1755, Pt II, Bk iii (*bis*) pp. 61–4.

of wig, the wearing and turning of hats, the shape of shoes and buckles. In the Parade we come to distinguish the wealthy physicians with their gold canes, the lawyers, and 'citizens' who are the merchants and traders of the City, not only by their being apart from the ultra-fashionables, but by details of dress, their wigs, in particular. Dr Johnson defined a 'cit' in his Dictionary as 'a pert low townsman; a pragmatical trader;' but this is one of his light-hearted definitions. Leading cits have the all-important 'Esquire' after their names and their heiresses contribute rich dowries to the impecunious among the nobility and gentry.[36] They have their own society, the society of the great City Companies, the Goldsmiths, Fishmongers, Skinners, etc., whose origins go back to the Middle Ages and whose wealth is enormous. They sit in Parliament and take an active part in the growing charitable enterprises of London: St George's Hospital, 'for the relief of poor, sick, and disabled persons,'[37] the Foundling Hospital, 'for exposed and deserted children,'[38] the London Infirmary, 'for the relief of all sick and diseased persons, and particularly manufacturers, seamen in the merchant service, and their wives and children,'[39] the Middlesex Hospital, 'for the sick, lame, and

36. Cf. L. B. Namier, *England in the Age of the American Revolution*, 1930, pp. 9–15, for a brilliant passage on 'The Upper Classes.'

37. Founded in 1733.

38. Founded in 1739; opened in 1745.

39. Founded in 1740.

cancer patients.'[40] But the eighteenth century is composed of castes and these worthies rarely join the smartest supper-parties at Ranelagh, or anywhere else.

If we go down from our place in the gallery at Ranelagh, by benefit of the magic which has made these tours possible, and mingle with the Parade, what do we hear? The preliminaries of the Peace have given offense to the City who disapprove making grants of money to the Pretender; the Princess of Wales has the jaundice; Sir Harry Calthorp has gone mad and walked down Pall Mall with the red ribbon of the Bath tied about his hair. There is no end of gossip: about great gambling losses; about the alleged impotence of the newly married Admiral Anson. (Methodism has not yet curbed the freedom of speech of the fashionable world.) We hear the latest bon-mots of George Selwyn and Lady Townshend, which give us in no time the tone of mixed society. George the Second is on his way to Hanover, accompanied by his mistress, the Countess of

40. Founded in 1745. *The Gentleman's Magazine*, May 1748, xviii. 198, reports: The Numbers of Objects under Cure the last Year in the Several Hospitals and Infirmaries of this Metropolis.

St Bartholomew's hospital	7,193
St Thomas's hospital	7,243
Bethlem hospital	403
Bridewell hospital	401
St George's hospital	5,436
Westminster infirmary	2,336
Mr Guy's hospital	2,242
London hospital, or infirmary	7,298
Total	32,552

Yarmouth, and in that circumstance alone we see what a gulf the Victorian Age is to dig between the eighteenth and twentieth centuries.

Of the appalling conditions of life at the other end of the town we naturally hear nothing. The gentlemen of the Parade are on the boards of the new charities and all make frequent contributions to release debtors from their confinement and to reward 'the deserving poor,'[41] but the welfare of the mob is, of course, chiefly a matter of concern to merchants. That 'the poor should be kept strictly to work and that it was prudent to relieve their wants, but folly to cure them,'[42] is as sound doctrine in 1748 as it was when Mandeville propounded it in 1714.

Duelling is still common, we learn with dismay; one must be prepared to protect one's ego (which is called 'honour' in the eighteenth century) with sword or pistol. We find the Parade violently concerned with the duel between Lord Coke, son of the Earl of Leicester, and Harry Bellenden. It took place on the 28th of June 1748 in Marylebone Fields in a mist and without casualty. The quarrel sprang directly out of a drinking bout between Coke and Bellenden, but its origins went further back. Coke had married the celebrated eccentric known as Lady Mary Coke, daughter of John Campbell, Duke of Argyll, but Lady Mary, as the world well knew, was wife in name only. When

41. See W. S. Lewis and Ralph M. Williams, *Private Charity in England, 1747–1757*, New Haven, 1938.

42. Bernard Mandeville, *The Fable of the Bees*, 1714.

her father-in-law, Lord Leicester, understood that this was the case he had her locked up in his house in Norfolk. Bellenden is connected with the Campbells by marriage, and, indeed, it is said by the Coke supporters that the Campbells had set Bellenden on to murder Coke. The Cokes further declare that when, at the duel, Coke had fired his last shot, Bellenden stepped up to him saying, 'You little dog, now I will be the death of you,' and fired, but his pistol failed to go off, in the merciful manner of eighteenth-century pistols. Everybody has taken sides according to whether they are Whigs, as are the Cokes, or Tories, as are the Campbells, and we have an uneasy sense of visiting a world where bad blood between friends may expend itself in Marylebone Fields instead of, as in the twentieth century, at one's desk where one writes a letter which, if he is wise, he does not send.

The fashionable gentlemen at Ranelagh have a club of their own, White's, in St James's, the first modern club and unique in 1748. The rest of the metropolis look upon it with horror because of its high gambling, but the rest of the metropolis also have places of resort, the coffee-houses and the taverns. The coffee-house is where one may talk politics, read the ten London newspapers of the day,[43] where one's letters may be addressed, where

43. For a list of them and the seventy-three other newspapers and periodicals printed in Britain in 1748, see Ronald S. Crane and Fred B. Kaye, *A Census of British Newspapers and Periodicals*, 1620–1800, Chapel Hill, 1927, p. 188.

one makes appointments, and where one may meet others of one's trade or profession. Lloyd's in the City is such a coffee-house for those interested in shipping and foreign trade; booksellers meet at The Chapter off Paternoster Row, medical men at Batson's in Cornhill.[44] The Bedford in Covent Garden and George's near Temple Bar are the literary ones. 'My next care,' wrote Roderick Random after taking lodgings near Charing Cross on his return from France, 'was to introduce myself into a set of good acquaintance; for which purpose I frequented a certain coffee-house, noted for the resort of good company, English as well as foreigners, where my appearance procured all the civilities and advances I could desire.'[45] This is the course followed by the eighteenth century, in fact and in fiction, and it is noteworthy that in spite of eighteenth-century ceremony introductions in the meeting places are effected as easily as they are in the less formal sections of twentieth-century America. No aspect of eighteenth-century life surprises us more than this. Men shake hands until the 'shoulder is almost dislocated.'[46] They ceremoniously doff their hats to each other. Tears are shed by men through rage or emotion in a manner not considered manly since the great ice age of the nineteenth century covered the Anglo-Saxon race. The Latin element in the English

44. 'The dispensers of life and death, who flock together, like birds of prey, watching for carcasses, at Batson's.' (*The Connoisseur*, 31 Jan. 1754.)
45. Smollett, *Roderick Random*, 1748, chapter XLV.
46. Grosley, i. 90.

character relieves itself in many ways familiar to twentieth-century travellers in Latin countries, the most embarrassing of which is in such evidence, even in the West End, that none other than Casanova is going to be revolted by it in 1763.[47] Seventeen hundred and forty-eight goes still further: it empties the contents of its portable plumbing out the window without warning whenever it feels like it. Eighteenth-century London is not embarrassed by a necessity of nature; and it does not open its windows at night.

The taverns range from the respectable Turk's Head and the Mitre, which Dr Johnson and The Club are to make famous, to alehouses where the prevailing insecurity of the age expresses itself without legal or moral restraint. In these places clubs meet whose members are of similar occupations or interests. There are clubs for actors or those who would be actors, for doctors and lawyers, clubs to hold lotteries, and clubs for thieves, and prostitutes. Drinking and gambling are as excessive here as elsewhere and the snuff of the fashionable world is supplemented by churchwarden pipes, a form of smoking which is to carry a taint of the 'low' for two centuries.

47. *Memoirs*, ed. Arthur Machen, 1928, ix. 234–5. Casanova does not give a date in the account of his London sojourn, but, in spite of anachronisms which may be the fault of the text and not of Casanova's memory, the year is clearly 1763. The question is settled by Horace Bleackley in *Notes and Queries*, 10th and 11th Series (1907–12); see also his *Casanova in England* [1923]. The British technique was to turn towards the middle of the street instead of towards the wall. Malcolm, *Anecdotes*, 1810, ii. 402, delicately hints at the same procedure.

The coffee-houses, taverns, and alehouses are not the only places of entertainment. His Majesty's Bear Garden, Hockley-in-the-Hole, Clerkenwell, may provide the spectacle of a dog dressed up with fireworks over him turned loose to fight a man,[48] or it may put on a fight between two women stripped to the waist, 'each woman holding half-a-crown in each hand, and the first woman that drops her money' loses the battle.[49] Other refinements of pleasure may be seen all over London as set forth in Hogarth's 'Four Stages of Cruelty,' but as we hurry over them even in the prints we fly from them in fact.

Less distressing and equally typical of the eighteenth century are the 'Exhibitions' of curious animals and people, what a later age is to call 'freaks': dwarfs, giants, learned horses, dogs, and geese; a North American savage, American elk, Bengal tigers, the real unicorn or rhinoceros, all to be seen for a shilling. At the Heathcock at Charing Cross is a mermaid,[50] and during Bartholomew Fair in August we may visit 'a wonderful and surprising satyr at the first house on the Pavement from the End of Hosier Lane.'[51]

We go to the theatre half a dozen times and see Garrick and Quin, Kitty Clive and Mrs Pritchard,

48. Alexander Andrews, *The Eighteenth Century*, 1856, p. 60, quoting an advertisement of Sept. 1730, of 'an entertainment' at Hockley-in-the-Hole.

49. Wheatley, Henry B., *London Past and Present*, ii. 217.

50. *Daily Advertiser*, 2 July 1748.

51. Ibid., 24 Aug. 1748.

but the account of the theatre must wait. What is more entertaining than any of the professional entertainments is London itself, the endless fascination of the streets, the parks, the shops, and the River. 'On Monday last,' writes *Old England* on 6 August 1748, 'as the Company of Vintners were going up the River a Swan-Upping, according to annual Custom, they saw their Royal Highnesses the Prince and Princess of Wales, in their Barge[52] going to Kew; on which Sir Daniel Lambert and the Court of Assistants sent a Message to acquaint them, that they did themselves the Honour to drink their Royal Highnesses Healths; hereupon the Prince ordered his Barge to fall in between that in which the Company were, and another that held their Ladies; in which Situation they continued for near two Hours, during which Time their Royal Highnesses conversed with them in the most affable Manner. Soon after the Barges joined, Prince George, Prince Edward, and Princess Augusta, came down in their Barge, and went on board that of their Royal Father; the Company then drank their Healths, which was most obligingly returned by that Illustrious Family; who also drank Success to Trade, Prosperity to the City of London, the Worshipful Company of Vintners, their Ladies, &c. While this was doing his Royal Highness sent the Ladies Sweatmeats, Pine Apples, Burgundy, and Cham-

52. This was presumably not his 'Chinese' barge, nor were the rowers in Chinese habits, as described in *The Gentleman's Magazine*, 1749, p. 377.

paign; and the Gentlemen, Claret; in fine, after spending this Time with his accustomed Freedom and Good-Nature, he took his leave in the most genteel Manner; and was pleased to order ten Guineas to be given to the Company's Watermen.'

Home again in the twentieth century what are our impressions of 1748? We have a thousand mental pictures, which are the most perishable of all pictures, but as time goes by they fade into a single picture, a surrealist picture, made up of symbols: a sedan chair, wide hoops, a grenadier in his high hat, London Bridge with its houses, heavy furniture and plate, landscape gardening made to look as much as possible like paintings by Claude or Poussin or Salvator Rosa. We think of Devis and Hogarth, of Horace Walpole deciding to remodel Strawberry Hill in the Gothic style. We think of two books printed in the year, *Roderick Random* and Dodsley's *Collection*. In the latter, among poems by Shenstone, Dyer, and Lyttelton appear three odes by a newcomer who is to exceed even Pope in popularity, Thomas Gray. One of these odes ends

> *where ignorance is bliss,*
> *'Tis folly to be wise,*

a sentiment popular in the eighteenth century and one much quoted since by moralists and the comfortably fixed.

We think of the dark background of 1748, of

the babies thrown, literally, on the dung hills and then we think of Captain Coram and the Foundling Hospital established to lessen the performance of so horrible a crime. The indifference of 1748 to religion was great; the eighteenth-century's throat did not tighten, as had its predecessor's, when it saw a spire rising across the fields;[53] protestantism had no longer to be fought for. Yet in 1748 the Wesleys and Whitefield were preaching to the poor and their words were to revolutionize society, even though the gentlemanly wars of the eighteenth century did not try the souls of men. The wars were economically disturbing: disbanded soldiers and sailors have always been a problem, and the national debt did mount rapidly,[54] but eighteenth-century collectors who, as a group, have never been surpassed, did not have to give up the purchase of a single picture or book or 'natural curiosity' for lack of money. The footmen of the great still wore liveries which cost many times their year's wages.

'Every country and every age has dominant terms, which seem to obsess men's thoughts,' writes Professor Namier.[55] 'Those of eighteenth-century England were property, contract, trade, and profits. Locke, its teacher, declared that "government has no other end but the preservation of

53. See *The New Statesman and Nation*, 2 Nov. 1940, p. 446, 'Books in General,' by V. S. Pritchett.

54. It was £78,000,000 in 1748; £257,000,000 in 1783.

55. L. B. Namier, *England in the Age of the American Revolution*, p. 36.

property,"[56] but under the term "property" he included a man's "life, liberty, and estate." '

The phrase has a familiar ring, but the difference is significant. Locke wrote 'estate' and not 'pursuit of happiness.' By 'estate' he meant man's status or position in society, a man of property, of course. The concept of the pursuit of happiness was to come about during the next quarter century and was to be propounded in the New World. Anyone who had talked about 'the mob' enjoying the pursuit of happiness as a principle of government would have been unintelligible in 1748; but the mob could make the great light up their houses and put down their carriage windows when they demanded either, and when they did so the great acknowledged the mob's right to shout as one of the inalienable rights of all free-born Englishmen.

56. John Locke, *Civil Government*, 1690.

A TOUR THROUGH LONDON

1776

1776

THERE is a particular pleasure in revisiting a city where one has spent some time. If, just before returning to it, you think of earlier visits, you are surprised to discover what trivial things you remember. When I think of my own twentieth-century visits to London I first think of the smell of coal smoke. I find this an extraordinarily pleasant smell, for one that sounds so unpleasant, since it brings back more than anything else does the experience of being in London in those days: it makes me think, why I can't say, of the crowds hurrying along the dreary eastern end of Oxford Street in the rain; of going to the theatre and walking down long flights of carpeted stairs to reach one's seat in the stalls. At the foot of the stairs lurking behind a portière waited the usher with a large black bow in her hair. She was always very refined and had false teeth and sold programmes for six-pence, but failed, for all her worldliness, ever to sell me the box of chocolates she had under her arm. I remember the door in the smoking room at Brown's Hotel which sighed reprovingly when it shut and the cloistered atmosphere of that room where one lay back in a black leather arm-chair and read *The Times* with one's mouth open. I remember the almost unbearable excitement of the bookshops with their long, grave, discussions of the eighteenth century and the smell of coal smoke almost, but not quite, yielding to the smell of the books. I remember one late afternoon in the Brompton Road when, for a moment, the sun actually shone and the grime on the buildings turned to silver. These, I find, are what I think of first, rather than the people I met or any specific thing I did, or who was Prime Minister, or what was being done about housing in Poplar; but I was not as conscientious a tourist then as I have since become.

Now, as we return to London in 1776, we are curious, and a little apprehensive, about the changes of the past twenty-eight years. The old woman at the top of St James's Street from whom we bought flowers will have died. Miss Ridley is no more, and we shall miss her stories of the quality who used to lodge with her. Our 1748 coachman may be about, but even if he is his horses, Bully and Tortoise, will not be. (Knowing eighteenth-century horses by name had its own special charm. Our coachman had formerly been in Lord Gower's stables and had named his horses for two of Lord Gower's winners at Newmarket. It was all very personal.)

London itself will have changed. For one thing, the houses on London Bridge have been pulled down and Westminster and Blackfriars Bridges have been opened. It is odd how landmarks become personal and how we instinctively resent any change in them. We know we shall find many changes, some of them obvious, some of them subtle. The American War, as our Revolution is called, will affect London in many ways. One change will be immediately evident: the appearance of the Hulks in the River, the ships to which convicts are sent instead of to America. Moreover, we shall see dozens of our loyalist countrymen in the streets, a miserably unhappy lot whose money is running out and who bitterly resent the condescension of their hosts.

The American War, we are to find, is far more in the public mind than we had supposed it would be. The name of General Washington is becoming as familiar as that of Benjamin Franklin. Large sections of the public do not like the war at all; the City is opposed to it and so are the Whigs. As early as August 1775 'the man at the inn' at Canterbury told Walpole that the trade of the town was greatly 'decayed' by the war and that he used to get the astonishing figure of £200 a year from American tourists alone.[1] England is in the midst of its Second Civil War, and even though the battlefields of it are in America, we shall find little enthusiasm in London for it.

The American War is particularly disturbing, for since we were last here England has had one of the greatest years in her history—1759. In spite of their threat of invasion in flat-bottomed boats,

1. *Yale Edition of Horace Walpole's Correspondence*, ed. W. S. Lewis and W. H. Smith, New Haven, 1939, 7. 342.

the French were beaten all over the world, at Minden, Quiberon Bay, Quebec, Ticonderoga, Guadeloupe; and the names of Rodney, Hawke, Amherst, Granby, and Wolfe were added to the long roster of British heroes. Pitt's glory dazzled Europe; the bells of London wearied with ringing for victories. In the following year the old king died and his grandson, a model prince, came to the throne. But now, only sixteen years later, George the Third has failed to fulfill his youthful promise, and Lord North is not repeating the successes of '59.

We land at Bristol on the 29th of April and go to the White Lion Inn, where, as we know, Dr Johnson and Boswell are to dine, and where Johnson is to make a scene and send away the white bread as unfit to eat.[2] No two figures of the eighteenth century are more familiar to us than are these two: Johnson's great bulk, rolling head and gait, and near-sightedness; Boswell's eagerness and seeming self-importance. I wish I might tell you that we managed to join them at their table, that Boswell, discovering we were Americans, enjoyed Johnson's horror at being at the same table with us, and then what happened when it came out that we were twentieth-century Americans and were cross-examined on 1941. 'Sir,' I wish I could report Johnson thundering as we babbled on about the scientific wonders of the twentieth century, 'what manner of vessel is a

2. Boswell, *Life*, iii. 50.

thermos bottle?' But nothing of the sort happened, for the best of reasons: the magic is not strong enough, and we must leave the pair to discuss Chatterton's forgeries without their knowing what would have interested them more than anything else they encountered in their entire lives, the fact that they had been in the presence of posterity.

We like the White Lion no better than Johnson and Boswell do and hurry on to Bath. After a night in the most delightful of English provincial towns, we take to the Bath Road. The travelling is easier than it was on the Dover Road in 1748, for our carriage is a new model and has springs, and the roadway itself has been improved. However, we are ready to break our journey at the inn at Spine Hill near Newbury, after fifty miles and with sixty more to go. Lord Denbigh, Lord Mulgrave, the wicked and fascinating Lord Sandwich, and the famous Joseph Banks happen to be here also with two or three ladies of pleasure to enjoy 'the trouting season.' Lord Sandwich is First Lord of the Admiralty and, with the Empire breaking up, there are those who think he might be more gainfully employed, but here at Spine Hill he has caught 'trouts near twenty inches long,' and he has no intention of returning to Whitehall for two or three weeks,[3] a declaration of independence which is to be frequently reasserted by him and by other ministers during the next few years. It is

3. David Hume to William Strachie, 5 May 1776.

noteworthy that the survival of the more famous Declaration of Independence is in part due to the fact that a few men in vital cabinet posts in the 1770's would permit nothing to interfere with their pleasures.

The approach to London from the west involves crossing Hounslow Heath whose row of occupied gibbets does not deter candidates for the gibbets temporarily not in use. In spite of the death penalty and the impressment of vagabonds into service for the American War, robberies have never been so frequent, a circumstance ascribed by Walpole to 'the enormous dissipation of all orders of men,' and 'the outrageous spirit of gaming' which has 'spread from the fashionable young men of quality to the ladies and to the lowest rank of the people.'[4] The coaches of ladies and gentlemen are attended by armed servants, and the return home after dark from dinner in the smart suburbs of Richmond, Twickenham, and Kingston is as exciting as a dash across No Man's Land. When one ventures out without an armed guard it is prudent to take two purses, one of them filled with bad money or small change to turn over to the robber.[5]

The outlying villages of Hammersmith, Kensington, and Knightsbridge have grown, although there are still open fields between them. Walpole, who takes this road to get to his house at Twick-

4. Horace Walpole, *Last Journals*, ed. A. Francis Steuart, 1910, i. 545.

5. See Casanova, ix. 170; Walpole to Lady Ossory, 7 Oct. 1781; Archenholz, ii. 80.

enham, writes on the 17th of July 1776: 'Rows of houses shoot out every way like a polypus; and so great is the rage of building everywhere, that, if I stay here [at Strawberry Hill] a fortnight, without going to town, I look about to see if no new house is built since I went last. America and France must tell us how long this exuberance of opulence is to last! . . . This little island will be ridiculously proud some ages hence of its former brave days, and swear its capital was once as big again as Paris, or—what is to be the name of the city that will then give laws to Europe—perhaps New York or Philadelphia.'[6] These two themes, the American War and luxury, are dominant in 1776.

Luxury is not confined to the well born. Successful tradesmen formerly content to live over their shops now have a second house in the newer squares, a carriage and a footman.[7] Walpole puts the blame for the universal extravagance upon the East India Company who 'starved millions in India by monopolies and plunder, and almost raised a famine at home by the luxury occasioned by their opulence, and by that opulence raising the prices of everything, till the poor could not purchase bread!'[8] Johnson characteristically ap-

6. To Mann.

7. William E. H. Lecky, *A History of England in the Eighteenth Century*, 1887, vi. 185. See the references given there. Walpole records in his *Paris Journals*, 5 Sept. 1771, that the landlady of the Fountain at Canterbury 'came out with a large sprig of false diamonds in the front of her hair—very new luxury.' (*Yale Edition of Horace Walpole's Correspondence*, New Haven, 7-342.)

8. Walpole to Mann, 9 April 1772.

proves of the extravagance and subscribes to Mandeville's theory of 'private vices, public benefits.'[9] In these opposing views of Walpole and Johnson we see the paling lights of ancient Whig and Tory doctrines.

The outskirts of London are not pleasant. The chains of smoking brick-kilns that surround London are 'like the scars of the smallpox.'[10] Hogs root among garbage heaps. The charming churches are not so charming on closer inspection, for many of them have in their graveyards 'poor holes' which 'once opened are not covered till filled with dead bodies. . . . How noisome the stench is that arises from these holes so stowed with dead bodies, especially in sultry seasons and after rain,' is too evident.[11] The professors and students at the new anatomical lectures, conducted by John and William Hunter, are grateful for this accessibility, but we are glad to pass through the turnpike at Hyde Park Corner and get to Arlington Street where, during this tour, we are to stay at Horace Walpole's house. (How this was brought about is a matter too dark to be disclosed.) Our host is at Strawberry Hill, but he has left a maid to take care of us. We have passed the house many times in the twentieth century, when it is to face the Ritz.

In the short ride from Hyde Park Corner to

9. Boswell, *Life*, iii. 55.

10. Jonas Hanway, quoted by George, *London Life*, p. 98.

11. *Some Customs Considered Whether Prejudicial to the Health of This City*, 1721, pp. 7–10, quoted by George, *London Life*, p. 353. See also, *The Gentleman's Magazine*, 1776, p. 302.

Arlington Street we have seen many new stone houses[12] and the benefits of the Westminster Paving Act of 1762[13] have been immediately evident. There are new gutters on each side of the street, instead of the kennel in the middle of it; footways, or as we should say, sidewalks, have been laid and the old posts removed; doorsteps no longer jut into the footway and force the pedestrian into the street. The picturesque and dangerous signs have gone and numbers have appeared on shop fronts. Millis & ffossick, At the Black Horse are now Number '9 opposite ye church in Crooked Lane.'[14] Flat stones have replaced the small pebbles of the street itself and causeways raised above the level of it serve as crossings for foot passengers, to the discomfort of those in carriages.[15] As a result of the paving, apprentices are less busy washing the fronts of houses bedaubed with mud from the wheels of carriages, and the trade of shops dedicated to scouring clothes has been somewhat diminished, although they are still indebted to London's pall of smoke.[16] Further

12. 'I stared today at Piccadilly like a country squire; there are twenty new stone houses: at first I concluded that all the grooms that used to live there had got estates and built palaces.' (Walpole to Montagu, 8 Nov. 1759.)

13. *Commons Journals*, 1762, vol. 29, pp. 233, 255, 279.

14. From an invoice dated 17 May 1771 in Sir Ambrose Heal's collection. It is interesting to note that the Millis & ffossick invoice referred to *ante* page 16 is dated Nov. 28, 1762, the year of the Act establishing numbers on houses. Is is also interesting to note that on the second invoice Mr ffossick has become Mr Fossick and that 'the' has reverted to 'ye.'

15. Grosley, *A Tour to London*, 1772, i. 33.

16. Ibid. i. 34, 47.

proposals for improving the streets were submitted to Parliament on the 13th of March this year: That the congestion be relieved by the elimination of building materials, by the regulating of the open holes for letting down coal into the houses. It was recommended that the driving of cattle, casks, and carriages on the foot-pavement be stopped, together with the custom of throwing at 'oranges and other things, or at cocks, pigeons, and other fowls.' The making of bonfires and the letting off of gunpowder in the streets was likewise deprecated.[17]

In our walks about London we discover with dismay that eight of the ancient City gates have been taken down because 'under the alterations in the art of war' the gates 'could be of no present security to the inhabitants, and their heavy construction standing across the streets obstructed the free current of air.'[18] Only Newgate and Temple Bar remain and upon the top of Temple Bar there is now only one Rebel head, the second head having fallen down in 1772.[19] 'Old' London is gradually disappearing, for many of the older houses in the poorer quarters do not wait to be demolished, but fall down without warning, due to their being built of bricks which have been

17. *Commons Journals*, 13 March 1776. Quoted by George, *London Life*, p. 352.

18. John Noorthouck, *A New History of London*, 1773, p. 399; see also the plate of the gates between pp. 540 and 541 and p. 398 n. for the schedules referred to in the Act of 33 George II, c. 30 for widening the streets and passages in London.

19. See Boswell, *Life*, ii. 238, n. 3.

mixed with 'the slop of the streets, ashes, scavengers' dirt and everything that will make the brick earth and clay go as far as possible.'[20] Of new buildings the most notable are those designed by the Adam brothers, the Adelphi and Lansdowne House.

Foreigners now find London the most brilliantly lighted city in Europe. 'The lamps, which often consist of two, three, and sometimes four branches, are enclosed in crystal globes, and, being attached to iron supporters, are placed at a small distance from each other. They are lighted at sunset, both in winter and summer, as well when the moon shines as not [a startling innovation]. In Oxford Street alone, there are more lamps than in all Paris.'[21] It must be confessed, however, that these lamps are below twentieth-century standards. They consist of a small tin vessel, half filled with the worst oil, that the parochial authorities . . . can purchase at the lowest price to themselves and the highest charge to the rate payers. In this fluid fish-blubber is a piece of cotton twist which forms the wick, and as the globes are semi-opaque the light barely reaches to the middle of the street.[22] The link-boys have not lost their employment.

20. *London Chronicle*, 2 June 1764, quoted by George, *London Life*, pp. 74, 345.

21. Archenholz, *A Picture of England*, 1789, i. 135. See also, Grosley, i. 40–1, for a somewhat less enthusiastic description.

22. J. Richardson, *Recollections*, 1856, i. 31; quoted by George, *London Life*, p. 102.

During the day we are struck by the increased opulence of London. The carriages of the great are more numerous and magnificent than they were twenty-eight years ago.[23] The shops are even more fascinating, the shop-keepers are masters of an even more elegant cringe. 'Such men! so finical, so affected!' exclaims Evelina, 'they seemed to understand every part of a woman's dress better than we do ourselves.'[24] We spend a good deal of time at the china shop a few doors from our house at the corner of Piccadilly buying the new manufactures, Wedgwood, Spode, Crown Derby, and Lowestoft. It is particularly pleasant to visit Strahan and Cadell's and to get two of their new books uncut and in their original boards, Gibbon's *Decline and Fall of the Roman Empire* and Adam Smith's *Wealth of Nations*. (We salve our consciences for our extravagance in the eighteenth-century spirit by giving money to the beggars who still swarm the streets. Over a thousand poor continue to starve to death in London during the year.[25] The story of Dr Johnson putting pennies into the hands of destitute children sleeping in doorways is perhaps the truest picture of the time which can be drawn.[26])

Used as we are to eighteenth-century dress, the

23. See the eloquent complaint of Verax in *The Town and Country Magazine*, 1776, p. 377.

24. Fanny Burney, *Evelina* (first published 1778), edn 1920, p. 21.

25. Boswell, *Life*, iii. 401: 'Not absolutely of immediate hunger, but of the consequences of hunger.'

26. Birkbeck Hill, *Johnsonian Miscellanies*, 1897, ii. 250.

'The Preposterous Head-Dress
or the Feathered Lady'

present mode makes us stare. The coats of the men are shorter and cut farther back than they were in 1748; the sleeves are tighter and the cuffs smaller; the collars are higher and lapels have appeared; the waistcoats are shorter; but men's clothes still cost a small fortune.[26a] The macaronis, the heirs of the petits-maîtres and the ancestors of the dudes, run to enormous cut steel buttons and walking sticks 'as long as leaping-poles,'[27] but it is the head-dresses of the women which eclipse anything seen before or since on a woman's head. Conservative ladies are content with a coiffure only a foot or two high and on top they limit themselves to scarves, an ostrich feather or two, and perhaps a rope of pearls, but the more imaginative build their heads up higher still and add flowers, herbs, and fruit. Hannah More, a moralist from her cradle, describes 'eleven damsels' at dinner, who 'had amongst them, on their heads,

26a. *A Catalogue of the Superb Household Furniture . . . of The Hon. Mr* Damer, *dec. at His Late Mansion in Tilney Street, May Fair . . . which will be sold by Auction by Mess. Christie and Ansell on the Premises . . . February the 3d*, 1777, *and the nine following days*, included Damer's wearing apparel, nos XLV–XLVII, pp. 34–7. Nos XLV and XLVII listed 34 'frocks,' coats, and 'suits,' and 56 waistcoats. Some of these were of washable materials, more were not, e.g. lot 14 in no XLVII: 'an Orlean frock lin'd with silk and steel buttons, a spotted velvet Manchester waistcoat and breeches and a buff waistcoat.' No XLVI was divided into ten lots which included 36 pair of silk stockings, 37 pair of worsted and thread stockings, and nine pair of socks.

The Quakers were a conspicuous exception to the prevailing extravagance of taste; 'their clothes, however, are generally made of the finest and choicest stuffs, though at the same time in a style of the greatest modesty' (St Fond, i. 116).

27. George Paston, *Social Caricature in the Eighteenth Century* [1905], p. 23.

an acre and a half of shrubbery besides slopes, grass-plats, tulip-beds, clumps of peonies, kitchen gardens, and green-houses.'[28] The erection of these works of art is, of course, not to be entered into lightly or unadvisedly.[29] The services of a skilled maid are essential, for after three hours of struggling with pomatum, powder, pins, combs, braids, and curling irons held high over her head with its cushion of wool rocking back and forth and her eyes straining into the mirrors which surround her a lady is no longer looking her best. Once the edifice has been raised, it must stand for days, and the night is not a season of repose. This is particularly the case when the edifice acquires tenantry of various types, the most unruly of which are mice.[30]

Two Acts passed since our last tour have had profound social consequences. The drinking of gin has been considerably reduced owing to the Act of 1751, which increased the tax on spirits and forbade their being sold retail by distillers, chandlers, and grocers. In 1748, you remember, a writer in *Old England* spoke of chandlers' shops debauching the poorest classes who went to the chandler to get bread, small beer, and cheese; 'the link boy

28. *Memoirs of the Life and Correspondence of Mrs Hannah More*, ed. William Roberts, 1834, i. 100. The year is 1777.

29. See James Stewart, *Plocacosmos: or the Whole Art of Hair Dressing*, 1782.

30. 'My cousin Mrs Coke was brought to bed of a dead child occasioned by a fright; a mouse got into her night-cap and demolished the heir to Holkham.' (Lady Mary Coke, unpublished journals in the possession of the Earl of Home, I Dec. 1776.)

went there for his nightly link, the servant maid to fetch soap or sand or candles';[31] both were treated to drams and their usefulness as servants rapidly vanished. Other salutary provisions in the law[32] made such changes that in 1776 Sir John Fielding, who has contributed as much as anyone to the improvement, believes, 'the rabble much mended within the last fifty years,' though, 'still very insolent and abusive . . . sometimes without the least appearance of a cause.'[33] We must not interpret the amendment as altogether a triumph of virtue, but rather as the triumph of the trading classes over the distilling interest. It was a triumph, that is, of one set of business men over another. The eighteenth century does not consider drunkenness a vice: Defoe said 'an honest drunken fellow is a character in a man's praise,' but he had in mind a man drunk on honest English ale. Throughout the century dozens of ministers of state, including first ministers, never went to bed sober. The mere thought of drinking three bottles of port in an evening turns the delicate stomach of the twentieth century, but that is the nightly ration of many male members of England's eighteenth-century ruling class. In the beginning of our 1748 tour I mentioned the refraction which ideas undergo when passing from one generation

31. George, *London Life*, p. 37.
32. Ibid. p. 333, n. 41.
33. *A Brief Description . . . of London*, 1776, p. xxiii, quoted ibid. p. 3. *The Dictionary of National Biography* quotes *The Public Advertiser* 6 Jan. 1777 to cast doubt on Fielding's authorship of the book.

to another. The most tolerant view in the twentieth century of excessive drinking is that it is a disease more psychological in origin than anything else. The eighteenth century, on the other hand, feels little pity for the victim of it, nor anger, nor moral concern. Drinking is a display of manliness and, according to Dr Johnson, a man is never happy in the present unless he is drunk.[34]

The second salutary Act was the Marriage Act of 1753. It provided for the publication of marriage banns and put an end to the clandestine marriages celebrated in the Fleet and elsewhere by disreputable parsons who performed the ceremony without a license. 'Entries in the Fleet registers could always, for a consideration, be forged, antedated or expunged. The practice was a direct incitement to bigamy, fictitious marriage for purposes of seduction, or marriage as a result of a drunken frolic. By persuasion, force, or fraud, women were taken to the purlieus of the Fleet, and there married, to be stripped of their fortune and deserted.'[35] Prospective brides and bridegrooms were sometimes literally set upon by the pretended Clerks and Registers in this business and were dragged away to some alehouse or brandy shop to be married, the impostors 'even,' as one witness puts it, 'on a Sunday stopping them as they go to Church, and almost tearing

34. Boswell, *Life*, ii. 351; Johnson, of course, did not approve of drunkenness.

35. George, *London Life*, p. 315.

their Cloaths off their Backs.'[36] Now in 1776 if a couple wishes to be married without the formality of the banns or parents' consent, they must dash away to Gretna Green just over the Scottish border.

What is guardedly called 'immorality' is not only universal throughout the eighteenth century but perfectly open as well. Prostitutes are everywhere in evidence, and 'their business is so far from being considered as unlawful, that the list of those who are any way eminent in this profession is publicly cried about the streets: the list, which is very numerous, points out their places of abode, and gives . . . the several qualifications for which they are remarkable. A new one is published every year, and sold under the piazza of Covent Garden, with the title of *The New Atlantis*.'[37] Gentlemen of the upper classes keep mistresses more or less openly. That their ladies are not without consolation is proved by the increasing number of divorces for what the eighteenth century calls, with unaccustomed lack of candour, criminal conversation. There is no divorce court: the husband brings an action for *Crim. Con.* against his wife's lover in the King's Bench and recovers damages. The husband then obtains in the Consistory Court of the Bishop of London a sentence of divorce from bed and board against his wife. Finally, a private Act of Parliament is passed.[38] A full account of the

36. A letter signed 'Virtuous' in the *Weekly Miscellany*, 1 March 1735.
37. Grosley, i. 55.
38. Sir Frank MacKinnon in *Johnson's England*, ii. 299–300.

proceedings in the King's Bench is published—and the whole world is at liberty to pore over the misconduct of Lady Bolingbroke, or the Duchess of Grafton, or Lady Sarah Bunbury, whose divorce passed its third reading in the House of Commons on the 14th of May 1776.[39] As likely as not the lady reappears in a day or two with her new husband, her garment only slightly dusty around the hem. Wives are not to benefit by such Acts of Parliament until 1801.

It is very definitely a man's world in which woman's chief rôle is biological. The sexes meet at Vauxhall and Ranelagh and at large assemblies where they dance minuets, but dining is not an occasion of mutual entertainment. The men are bored until the arrival of dessert, when the ladies and servants retire, and 'the room having been furnished with a certain necessary utensil,[40] they lean upon the table with their elbows, drink about and settle the affairs of the nation.'[41] 'Everyone has to drink in his turn, for the bottles make a continuous circuit of the table and the host takes note that everyone is drinking in his turn. After this has gone on for some time and mere thirst has become inadequate reason for drinking, a fresh stimulus is supplied by the drinking of "toasts"; that is to say, the host begins by giving the name of a lady; he drinks to her health and everyone is

39. *Commons Journals*, vol. 35, p. 792.

40. Its appearance distressed the young Duc de la Rochefoucauld; see *A Frenchman in England*, 1784, trans. S. C. Roberts, Cambridge, 1933, pp. 30–1. It was kept in the deep drawers of the sideboard.

41. Grosley, i. 151.

obliged to do likewise. After the host someone else gives a toast and everyone drinks to the health of everyone else's lady. Then each member of the party names some man and the whole ceremony begins again. If more drinking is required, fresh toasts are always ready to hand; politics can supply plenty—one drinks to the health of Mr Pitt or Mr Fox, or Lord North,'[42] although in good society no one drinks the health of that dangerous rascal, John Wilkes.

The sexes share one other occupation, and that is gambling. Even in Walpole's ultra-respectable set it is not at all uncommon for the elderly ladies and gentlemen to lose at loo or whist or quinze fifty or one hundred guineas at a sitting.[43] It would be rash to say what these sums represent in 1941, but it might be upwards of a thousand and two thousand dollars. Casanova discovered that it is an unpardonable solecism to pay in gold instead of with bank notes.[44] The men also play hazard and faro. Walpole speaks of Brooks's, the famous new Whig Club, 'where a thousand meadows and cornfields are staked at every throw, and as many villages lost as in the earthquake that overwhelmed Herculaneum and Pompeii.'[45] Charles James Fox's gambling debts when he was twenty-four were £140,000.

42. De la Rochefoucauld, loc. cit.

43. *The Morning Post*, 4 Sept. 1776, reports that at Chatsworth, the Duke of Devonshire's, the ladies lost £500 or £1000 a night (quoted by John Hampden, *An Eighteenth-Century Journal*, 1940, p. 314).

44. *Memoirs*, ed. Machen, ix. 166.

45. Walpole to Sir William Hamilton, 19 June 1774.

The government encourages gambling by state lotteries. Horse-racing is popular. Eight large meetings are held at Newmarket in 1776, and eighty-four elsewhere in England,[46] but the ingenuity of the age supplements the conventional opportunities for gambling provided by horses, cards, dice, boxing, and cock-fighting. The betting-books at White's and Brooks's record this sort of thing: 'Lord Worthington wagers Mr Cox ten guineas that Mr Garrick after the expiration of his engagement for this season [1776], shall within two years act again (for a friend, public charity, and by command of the King excepted),'[47] or that Lady So-and-so would give birth to an heir before Lord Somebody-else got a place at Court. Casanova, who was always being shocked in London, tells how he saw a crowd of people who seemed to be staring at something. His companion went up to the crowd and then returned, saying: 'That's a curious sight for you; you can enter it amidst your remarks on English manners.'

'What is it?' asked Casanova.

'A man on the point of death from a blow he has received in boxing with another sturdy fellow.'

'Cannot anything be done?'

'There is a surgeon there who would bleed him, if he were allowed.'

'Who could prevent him?'

'That's the curious part of it. Two men have betted on his death or recovery. One says, "I'll

46. *Baily's Racing Register*, 1845, i. 418–36.
47. *The History of Whites*, 1743 *to* 1878, ii. 40.

bet twenty guineas he dies," and the other says, "Done." Number One will not allow the surgeon to bleed him, for if the man recovered, his twenty guineas would be gone.'[48]

This is the sort of thing that shocks us, as well as Casanova, in the eighteenth century, the sort of thing we have not prepared ourselves for. Many of the conditions of its daily life we have anticipated. We have known, for example, that the food would be odd, and part of our mental preparation for these tours was a course in shutting our minds to what we might be eating. This resolution is shaken on the 4th of May this year when we read in *The Public Advertiser:* 'The various horrid tricks practised on our meat, fish, etc., is shocking to think of. Meat inflated with the breath of distempered gin drinkers, the animal heated and bruised before slaughter by cruel treatment; all this is surely enough to render our food quite unwholesome, and at least sufficient to disgust the least delicate stomach . . . but,' and here we get again comment which is repeated over and over in 1776, 'but in this age of dissipation and amusement everything is immediately given up that will cost the least trouble to attain.'[49]

48. *The Memoirs of Jacques Casanova*, ed. Arthur Machen, 1928, ix. 234–5.

49. Grosley has a passage on the 'flabbiness' of English meat and fowl (i. 69–70). St Fond, on the other hand, found the meats 'plain, though exquisitely flavoured' (i. 36); when dining with the Royal Society, each person seasoned the meat 'as he pleased with the different sauces which were placed on the table in bottles of various shapes. The beef-steaks and the roast beef were at first drenched with copious bumpers of strong beer, called porter, drunk out of cylindrical pewter pots, which are much preferred to glasses, because one can swallow a whole pint at a draught' (St Fond, i. 47).

Although we don't understand what the writer means by 'inflating the meat,' we are thankful that we smuggled a little twentieth-century bicarbonate of soda into our luggage. Eighteenth-century dinners are an acquired taste. They are generous and they are unfamiliar. For example, a typical family dinner is a soup of green peas which is called a remove, because it is taken away when the next dish arrives. This is stewed carp and with it, as part of the course, are served beans and bacon, white fricassee of tripe, salad, and chine of veal. All this is called the first course. The second course consists of roasted capons, veal sweetmeats, fried pasties of venison, tarts, and rabbits. The official name for this meal is 'Dinner: Five in a course.'[50] Casanova said, 'an English dinner is like eternity—it has no beginning and no end.'[51] It is eaten with two-pronged forks and knives with broad, curved ends. At our first meal we discover the usefulness of these knives and why one edge of them is rounded, for unless we overcome our twentieth-century prejudice against eating with a knife we shall fall rapidly behind the procession.

In spite of the vaccinations and paratyphoid injections we had before setting out on these tours, we remain uneasy about falling ill in the eighteenth century. If worst comes to worst we shall have to call in an apothecary who after seeing us will go to the coffee-house where he will find the physician

50. Harrison, Mrs Sarah, *The House-keeper's Pocket Book* [1783], p. 97.
51. *Memoirs*, ix. 67.

he is accustomed to consult. He will tell the physician our symptoms and the physician will write out directions in Latin for what is to be done. The apothecary will return to us when he has made up the prescribed clysters, purges, and emetics and he will bring a barber-surgeon if bleeding has been ordered. Only if we are at the extreme will the physician himself come.[52] As to the surgeons, even though Cheselden has succeeded in reducing the cutting for the stone to half a minute, a glimpse of the contents of a surgeon's kit in a shop window has revealed the agony of the operating table where the only anesthetic is a glass of brandy. The eighteenth century's tolerance of pain puts us of the twentieth century to shame. It is seldom necessary to bind patients to the table and although they sweat profusely, they rarely faint.[53] The London General Bill of Christenings and Burials shows us what we may catch besides a cold. The most common fatal diseases are 'convulsions,' 'consumption,' 'fever,' and smallpox, in that order. 'Teeth' is, rather surprisingly, high on the list, far outstripping 'apoplexy and sudden.' 'Grief' and 'rising of the lights' have been virtually conquered.[54]

Gout accounts for a certain number of appearances in the burials and gout is almost as much a staple of eighteenth-century conversation as the

52. Paraphrased from Sir D'Arcy Power in *Johnson's England*, ii. 272.
53. Ibid. ii. 269.
54. *The Gentleman's Magazine*, 1774, p. 611.

weather. It is at once common and mysterious. It is given a title, 'the.' Quacks flourish by it and all classes of society take their nostrums. The great object of its treatment is to drive it into the extremities, for if it settles in the head or stomach, all is over. Horace Walpole, a great authority on the gout, uses iced water and believes that a hard frost is efficacious in a cure. William Cole, on the other hand, an equally great authority, believes a frost hurries on the gout. No one, that is, knows what the gout is or just what you should do to conquer it, but everyone has his pet method of treatment. My own is the course prescribed to Horace Walpole by a great lady in Paris, who assured him that there was nothing so good for the gout as to preserve the parings of one's nails in a bottle close stopped.[55] The gout is a factor in the national life, not only because of its assaults upon leading ministers of state at moments of crisis, but because of its invasion of men's very souls. It is here and there, a spirit of fire, to be courted and cajoled, attacked and appeased. The eighteenth century is like Caliban crouching in terror as it waits for the gout to rack it with old cramps and fill all its bones with aches. But cruel and capricious as the gout is, it has one sovereign merit: it is jealous of all other diseases and drives them away. This is why we find the gout spoken of with a certain affection; but when Walpole talks about gout of the eyeball and gout of the face, we

55. Walpole to Gray, 19 November 1765.

suspect that other spirits have already moved in.[56]

The other distinctively eighteenth-century malady is the one which goes by many names: the hypochondria or the English malady; in men it is called the spleen, in women the vapours. Boswell's journals provide perhaps the most vivid account of it, but it periodically descends like a pall upon nearly everyone. Foreigners suggest that it comes from the fogs, the diet of meat and porter, the gloom of the Protestant religion and the laws against having any sort of good time on the Sabbath, and many other causes. When the spleen reaches its most extreme stage suicide follows and suicide is practised not only by the fashionable world but by all classes in the last half of the eighteenth century. There are those who recognize this for what it is, a disease of the soul,[57] and the Book of Common Prayer has a passage in its Visitation of the Sick for those who are troubled in mind.

Our tours are fortunately so short that we do not run much risk of the gout or the spleen, but we are in constant danger from what a writer in *The Gentleman's Magazine*[58] who signs himself 'Hygeia' calls 'the putridity of the air' in public

56. 'He [Walpole] said he considered the gout as a cure for other distempers, not as a distemper, and he would not be free of it if he could, for he knew how to manage it, he did not know how to manage other distempers; he thought it a kind of harlequin, for it often appeared in the shape of other complaints.' (James Boswell, *Private Papers*, ed. Geoffrey Scott and Frederick A. Pottle, New York, 1928–34, 17. 102.)

57. Archenholz, i. 177.

58. For July, 1776, pp. 302–4.

places. There are two new 'sights' since we were here in 1748, the British Museum and the Royal Academy, and we take our lives boldly in hand and see them.

The British Museum was opened to the public in 1759, in the same place tourists of the future are to know, for three hours a day. There is as much red-tape in making a visit of an hour to it as in securing the use of it in the twentieth century. Applications must be in writing and have to be approved, but no more than ten tickets are issued for each hour. After waiting for our hour to arrive in a reception room where the catalogue[59] states we cannot spend the time disagreeably because of the fine view from a window of the distant hills of Hampstead and Highgate, we are permitted to visit the three departments of manuscripts, coins, and medals, the natural curiosities, and the printed books. The Museum already has the Harleian manuscripts and the Cottonian and Royal Libraries, Sir William Hamilton's vases, and the great collections in all subjects formed by Sir Hans Sloane, whose enlightened will initiated the establishment of this repository of national treasure. The individual star-pieces which everyone must see are Magna Charta, the fourth-century Codex Alexandrinus, and Queen Elizabeth's prayer book written by herself, the red velvet cover of which has flowers worked by her own hands.

The Royal Academy Exhibition is in Pall Mall,

59. *The General Contents of the British Museum*, 1761, p. 12.

and, as we have been led to expect from the prints of it, the paintings are piled one on top of the other to the ceiling. The President, Sir Joshua Reynolds, dominates the exhibition with no less than thirteen portraits, including such familiar ones as those of the Duke and Duchess of Devonshire, Lord Althorpe, Master Herbert in the Character of Bacchus, Master Crewe in the Character of Henry the Eighth, and the portrait of Lord Temple which Walpole in his catalogue of the exhibition calls the finest portrait Reynolds ever painted.[60] Apart from these, however, the exhibition is disappointing. We have struck an off-year in the English School, whose recent establishment has been a source of such national pride. Gainsborough is not represented, nor Romney, whose fashionable clientele rivals Reynolds' own and for whom, as for Gainsborough, Reynolds has little good will. Hoppner, Lawrence, and Raeburn are still too young to appear. Our own Benjamin West, however, is present with four conversation pictures. Gilbert Stuart in 1776 is eking out a precarious existence as organist of St Vedast's in Foster Lane,[61] his name as yet unknown to artists. Loutherbourg and Paul Sandby contribute landscapes, and George Stubbs several animals. We feel we have discovered the Reverend Matthew

60. Algernon Graves, *The Royal Academy of Arts. A Complete Dictionary of Contributors*, 1906, vi. 272.

61. See William Dunlap, *A History . . . of the Arts of Design in the United States*, Boston, 1918, i. 203–4. Although the account there is based on hearsay, Mr John Hill Morgan assures me that it is undoubtedly correct.

William Peters whose delightful portraits of children have never received the recognition due them.

On the night of Monday the 10th of June the eighteenth-century theatre reached its climax when Garrick made his final appearance. We have managed to get places in a side box[62] and so have avoided 'suffering [the] thumps, squeezes, and almost suffocation' which proved more than our loyalist fellow-countryman, Judge Curwen of Boston, could endure[63] on his last visit to Drury Lane. Normally the doors open at five, the curtain rises at six; during the interval the orchestra plays three selections known as the First, Second, and Third Music, for the benefit of those in the pit and galleries who have already won places in the free-for-all seats after the doors open. Little can be heard, however, above the uproar of the audience fighting for seats and the bawling of the orange-women selling play-bills, tea and coffee, and an occasional orange at a shilling apiece.[64] On this night, however, the schedule is moved on half an hour and the play-bill[65] notes, 'Ladies are desired to send their servants a little after 5 to keep places, to prevent confusion.'

62. Single seats cost five shillings in a box, three in the pit, two in the first gallery, and one in the upper gallery, according to newspaper advertisements.

63. On the 4th of May when Garrick played Archer for the last time. (Samuel Curwen, *Journal and Letters*, New York, 1845, p. 55.)

64. Alwin Thaler, *Shakespere to Sheridan*, Cambridge, Mass., 1922, p. 220, quoting *The Conduct of the Four Managers of Covent-Garden Theatre, by a Frequenter of the Theatre*, 1768, pp. 18–19.

65. Reproduced in *Johnson's England*, ii. 173, and in John Hampden, *An Eighteenth-Century Journal*, 1774–76, 1940, p. 288.

Riot at Covent Garden, 1763

The changes at Drury Lane have been remarkable since 1748, changes in the house itself, in the stage, and in the audience. Garrick enlarged Drury Lane in 1762 to hold 337 guineas a night instead of 220, which is to say that Drury Lane now holds about two thousand people. Some ten years ago Garrick introduced the French technique of lighting the stage from behind the scenes and he did away with the six large rings which formerly hung over the stage, 'greatly to the advantage of the performers,' as *The Annual Register* observed,[66] 'but more to that of the spectators, who have now no longer the air they breathe tainted by the noxious smoke of between two and three hundred tallow candles, nor their sight obstructed by them and the rings supporting them.' There is still an apron upon which the actors advance at once on their entrance and Garrick still requires that those playing a scene with him shall turn their backs to the audience when addressing him so that there will be no question whatever of its attention being diverted from him. Failure to observe this rule during our 1776 tour caused young Mrs Siddons to fall into disfavour and contributed to her dismissal from the company.[67]

It must be confessed that our chief entertainment at eighteenth-century theatres has been laughing at them rather than with them, at the tragedies particularly, but there is less to laugh at

66. 1765, p. 130.
67. Thomas Campbell, *Life of Mrs Siddons*, 1834, i. 74–5.

in 1776 than there was in 1748; less bombast, better costuming, and more elaborate sets. *The Rivals*, which appeared a year ago, and *She Stoops to Conquer*, which appeared two years before that, help us to feel more at home with the plays. Only Garrick himself reminds us of 1748, with his burning eyes and astonishing 'universality,' to use the eighteenth century's own word for him.

Now in 1776 the curtain is raised and lowered during the course of the play and not merely at its close; so that an actor who loses his life in Act III is no longer under the painful necessity of rising after a decent interval and walking off under the gaze of the audience. The last scene of every act is still, however, constantly interrupted by the tinkling of a little bell which warns the music to be ready to play in the interval between the acts,[68] and a carpet is still brought out in the last act for Garrick and the principal actresses to die upon in the interest not only of their importance but of their clothes.[69]

Costuming has improved in 1776, but it still falls below twentieth-century requirements. In 1748 Banquo's ghost appeared in a tye wig (along with all the other gentlemen in the company), and the effect of Macbeth's 'never shake thy gory locks at me,' was considerably weakened.[70] Horace Walpole records with disapproval that the witches

68. Grosley, i. 178.

69. Odell, George C. D., *Shakespeare from Betterton to Irving*, New York, 1921, i. 413–4.

70. *An Essay on Acting*, 1744, quoted by Allardyce Nicoll, *A History of Late Eighteenth Century Drama*, 1750–1800, Cambridge, 1927, p. 36.

GARRICK AND MRS PRITCHARD IN *Macbeth*

in the same play 'are dressed with black hats and blue aprons, like basket women and soldiers' trulls, which must make the people not consider them as beings endowed with supernatural powers.'[71] The men's costumes have been the first to yield to historical accuracy, but managerial thrift has kept down expenses and all the men in the same play are not dressed in the same period of costume. The empresses and queens are still confined to black velvet, except on extraordinary occasions, when they put on an embroidered or tissue petticoat. The young ladies of the company appear in a cast-off gown of some person of quality.[72] The principal actresses 'drag long trains after them, which have four corners, like a carpet, the breadth proportioned to the importance of the character; and they are followed by a little boy, in quality of a train-bearer, who is as inseparable from them as the shadow from the body. This page, who is sprucely dressed, and muffled up in a livery, made to suit his stature within two or three inches, keeps his eye constantly fixed upon the train of the princess; sets it to rights when it is ever so little ruffled or disordered; and is seen to run after it with all his might, when a violent emotion makes the princess hurry from one side of the stage to the other: this he does,' as a foreign visitor says, 'with all the phlegm and seriousness

71. *Notes by Horace Walpole on Several Characters of Shakespeare*, ed. W. S. Lewis, Farmington, Ct, 1940, pp. 7–8.

72. *An Apology for the Life of George Anne Bellamy*, 1785, i. 130, quoted by Nicoll, op. cit. p. 37.

natural to the English,' a circumstance which, the same visitor points out, makes it difficult 'not to take notice of the attention of the little page, to repair the disorder, which the queen's train constantly receives, as she stirs and moves with impassioned attitudes in the arms of [her] afflicted monarch.'[73]

Since the importation of de Loutherbourg by Garrick in 1773, a revolution has been started in stage scenery. The old back drops and side wings are giving way to elaborate box sets and the sensitive playgoer is less offended by cracked and dingy canvas hopefully intended to suggest a palace or a wood. That the scene shifters do not always co-operate with the new spirit of realism is indicated by a critic who protests that 'we are often presented with dull clouds hanging in a lady's dressing-room, or . . . trees intermixed with disunited portions of the peristyle; vaulted roofs unsupported'[74]—but Rome was not built in a day.

The manners of the audience have improved since 1748, but the freedom of the audience to hiss and cat-call is still 'a branch of public liberty.'[75] No one is exempt from the feelings of the mob, for when the King himself appeared in one of the theatres after the additional tax was laid upon porter his 'ears were saluted . . . with all that indecent freedom of expression which the utmost

73. Grosley, op. cit. i. 178–9. Tate Wilkinson describes this same practice, iv. 88–9.

74. Dramaticus, in *The Gentleman's Magazine*, 1789, Pt I. 407.

75. Grosley, i. 54.

bitterness of resentment could suggest to a haughty people.'[76] The mob still is sovereign in the theatre, it makes and unmakes the plays and actors, and its privileges extend to rioting. Several serious riots have occurred since 1748. In 1763, for example, when the managers at Covent Garden tried to stop the long-established practice of admitting people at the end of the third act at half price, to see the two remaining acts and the two 'little pieces' which follow, the benches of the boxes and pit were torn up, the chandeliers broken, and the linings of the boxes were cut to pieces. The rioters tried to cut away the wooden pillars between the boxes to bring down the galleries, but, providentially, the inside of them was iron.[77] The offenders were not punished, although the theft of a handkerchief by one of them would have been sufficient to transport him for seven years.[78] The Theatre is a privileged place in the eighteenth century.

All witnesses of Garrick's last appearance agree that nothing so moving had been seen on any stage in or out of Christendom. He chose Mrs Centlivre's comedy, *The Wonder!*, a great favourite of his and of the public. The house was packed with the most fashionable audience ever gathered together in a theatre and when the play was over

76. Ibid. i. 55. See also Casanova, *Memoirs*, ix. 169.
77. *Annual Register*, 1763, p. 58.
78. By an Act of 1717 transportation for seven years was substituted for branding in the case of a larceny in which the convicted was able to claim 'Benefit of Clergy,' that is, could read. (Cf. Sir Frank MacKinnon in *Johnson's England*, ii. 304, n. 1.)

Garrick made a carefully prepared impromptu speech during which, at exactly the right moment, he burst into tears. More tears were then shed by the audience than ever were shed at a tragedy and the historic moment became one of the brightest pages in theatrical annals.[79]

Opera, both Italian and English, is as fashionable in 1776 as it was in 1748, but we find the performances of the Italian *castrati* embarrassing. Gay's *Beggar's Opera* and *Polly* continue to be unrivalled, so far as we are concerned, among eighteenth-century operas.[80] Handel's Oratorios which are often sung in church services compensate for the long theological sermons.

The eighteenth century has no end of music; ladies and gentlemen sing Purcell and Arne and play on the harpsichord and 'cello, the flute and harp. This they do in the spirit of earlier times and not with the self-conscious flutter of the nineteenth century. Musical parties on the Thames are popu-

79. The periodicals of the time are full of accounts of this occasion; George Colman the younger's being something less than sympathetic (see Richard Brinsley Peake, *Memoirs of the Colman Family* [1841], i. 404–8). Garrick's farewell appearance in *Lear*, when the characters were 'judiciously habited in old English dresses,' was so affecting that Regan and Goneril, 'forgetful of their characteristic cruelty, played through the whole of their parts with aching bosoms and streaming eyes.' *The Morning Post*, 22 May 1776, quoted by John Hampden, *An Eighteenth-Century Journal*, 1940, p. 280.

80. *The Morning Post*, 2 October 1776, complains of Mr Fisher's innovation at Covent Garden of having the airs in the *Beggar's Opera* accompanied 'only with a first and second fiddle, and Merlin's new forte piano': The results were 'more absurd, if possible, than the old style, of overpowering the voice with the full force of a large band.' (Quoted ibid. p. 319.)

lar, and at the most fashionable evening parties music may be provided, not only by professionals from the Opera, but by the ladies and gentlemen themselves. 'I was strolling in the garden,' writes Horace Walpole of Hampton Court, 'in the evening with my nieces, who joined Lady Schaub and Lady Fitzroy, and the former asked Mr Gammon to sing. His taste is equal to his voice, and his deep notes . . . are calculated for the solemnity of Purcell's music, and for what I love particularly, his mad songs and the songs of sailors. It was moonlight and late and very hot and the lofty façade of the palace and the trimmed yews and canal, made me fancy myself of a party in Grammont's time.'[81]

Nowhere is the spirit of 1776 more in evidence than at the innumerable masquerades. There were masquerades in 1748, but these of 1776 have taken on new life since their temporary banishment after the earthquake of Lisbon in 1755, which was interpreted as God's answer to the follies of the age. The present masquerades are given in many parts of the town, at Ranelagh, at Marylebone Gardens, and at the assembly rooms of the dictatress of fashionable entertainment, the celebrated Mrs Cornelys who is the mother of two of Casanova's children. Vast sums are spent on colonnades of glass, on orchestras of one hundred and fifty pieces, on fireworks and tight-rope dancers, on

81. Walpole to Lady Ossory, 11 August 1778, unpublished, in private hands.

representations of the boulevards of Paris with their shops, on 'rural scenes.' The masks run to tradesmen, with a sprinkling of harlequins—the usual conflict between realism and the romantic. Suppers are served of hot fowls and of chicken pies, cold hams and side dishes of fruit, together with port, Madeira, Lisbon, champagne, hock, and perry, and it is not to be wondered at that the conclusion of the masquerades is frequently unseemly.[82]

On May Day the milkmen and women and chimney-sweeps have a masquerade of their own. The milkwomen have an elaborate contraption they call a 'garland' which they trundle about the streets. The garland is a pyramid of seven or eight stories decked with flowers and herbs. At the corners of the pyramid, on each story of it, are pieces of silver, tea-kettles, salvers, urns, borrowed for the occasion and worth several hundred pounds. The sooty faces of the chimney-sweeps are whitened with meal, their heads covered with high periwigs, and their clothes decked out with ribbons and lace paper. They bang their brushes and scrapers together for all they are worth while the milkwomen dance and they get quite a little money for their pains.[83]

Such an eighteenth-century custom persists cheerfully in spite of the rise or fall of stocks or of

82. For accounts of masquerades see *The Town and Country Magazine* for June and July 1776, pp. 322–3, 342–3.

83. Grosley, i. 183–4; Samuel Curwen, *Journal and Letters*, New York, 1845, p. 54.

MAY-DAY IN LONDON

an interlude like the American War. The customs at the other end of the town proceed with an equal freedom from interruption; the war in America does not stop the playing of a single card, certainly not the announcement of the Declaration of Independence. This event is not chronicled in *The Annual Register*, which under the fourth of July merely records that on that day Governor Hutchinson of Massachusetts and his deputy, Peter Oliver, received honorary degrees at Oxford, but it is printed at length in *The Gentleman's Magazine*,[84] following an account of a lady and gentleman lately arrived from Siberia who are experts in hair-dressing. The news of the Declaration of Independence was received mournfully at the New England Coffee-House in Threadneedle Street where the American loyalists meet to read their letters from home and to hope that the colonists will teach the English a lesson.[85]

The supper parties of 1776 have had more entertaining things to talk about than the Americans. There has been the trial of the bigamous Duchess of Kingston, the thirty new Irish peers, the suicide of Mr Damer, and Omiah, the Tahitian savage whose grace, good looks, and dignity inspire the more intellectual to thoughts upon the perfectability of man and whether or not nature has some simple plan for his proper conduct.[86] The death of

84. August, 1776, pp. 361–2.
85. Samuel Curwen, *Journal and Letters*, New York, 1845, p. 90.
86. See Chauncey Brewster Tinker's delightful *Nature's Simple Plan*, Princeton, 1921.

Hume is probably the outstanding loss of 1776, but the fashionable assemblies think of him as an historian and secretary to Lord Hertford and General Conway. They discuss Mr Gibbon's *Decline and Fall of the Roman Empire*, for he is one of them, tapping his snuff-box in a way all his own, but there is no record of their applying to themselves a sentence on his opening page, 'Their peaceful inhabitants enjoyed and abused the advantages of wealth and luxury.' They do not discuss Dr Adam Smith's *Wealth of Nations*, which is much too hard reading. If they had, and if their lords and masters in Parliament had hearkened to his plea to give the Americans representation there, the history of the world would have been changed. They do not recognize the significance of the paragraph in *The Gentleman's Magazine* under date of July 10th which states that 'a riotous mob of weavers' in Somerset destroyed 'some machines lately erected there for expediting their work,' with the result that 'seven persons were either killed or wounded,'[87] and if anyone had said at one of the *conversazioni* conducted by Mrs Montagu or Mrs Vesey or dear Mrs Boscawen that this was the beginning of the Industrial Revolution, the phrase, of course, would not have been understood.

At the close of our 1748 tour I quoted Professor Namier to the effect that the words which ob-

87. *The Gentleman's Magazine*, 1776, p. 334.

sessed the eighteenth century were 'property, contract, trade, and profits.' He was speaking primarily of government. I might quote other authorities to show that the eighteenth century was obsessed, in other fields, with the words 'nature,' 'reason,' 'enlightenment.' The fact is, of course, that many words obsessed it, but if I were to choose one which seems to me to be the key word I would follow Professor Carl Becker's choice and pick out the word 'posterity.'[88]

Gibbon believed that mankind was emerging from the dark ages to enlightenment in the eighteenth century: The present is better than the past, the future will be better than the present. 'Whatever was the beginning of this world,' wrote Joseph Priestley, 'the end will be glorious and paradisaical, beyond what our imagination can now conceive.'[89] Diderot, as Professor Becker points out, substituted 'for the hope of immortality in heaven, the hope of living in the memory of future generations.'[90] This is the faith of our host in Arlington Street, Horace Walpole, who is a spokesman of his time and whose case is typical of its intellectuals. For him posterity offers the chance of salvation through his writings, but the oblivion of an unread book will be his intolerable fate should he fail. 'Those persons of future ages who will concern themselves with the past,' as he

88. See Carl Becker, *The Heavenly City of the Eighteenth-Century Philosophers*, New Haven, 1932.

89. Quoted ibid. p. 119.

90. Ibid. p. 149.

had concerned himself with the past, must find in him a safe guide to the eighteenth century. Posterity, the better time, became therefore, a daily concern. It was a judge whose awful verdict was to wait until the twentieth century to be pronounced. Posterity sat before him at his desk as he worked night after night for forty years, secretly, on his *Memoires*. Posterity was in the next room when he drafted and copied his matchless letters. Posterity, ourselves, stood silently in the shadows at Strawberry Hill while the eager quill scratched over the creamy paper.

In this hour of 1941, we have little time to think of posterity, and the perfectability of man is a bitter joke. When I began writing these lectures much of the London of our tours existed, but now that remnant has been greatly reduced. In so short a time has so much been lost. When the American War had become inevitable, Walpole wrote these words: 'The next Augustan age will dawn on the other side of the Atlantic. There will, perhaps, be a Thucydides at Boston, a Xenophon at New York, and, in time, a Virgil at Mexico, and a Newton at Peru. At last some curious traveller from Lima will visit England and give a description of the ruins of St Paul's.'[91]

91. Walpole to Mann, 24 Nov. 1774. This passage was later cribbed by Macaulay in his review of Ranke's *History of the Popes.*

A TOUR THROUGH LONDON

1797

1797

IT is a common practice among tourists to search for familiar comparisons on their tours. In Dorset we say, 'this is like the Mohawk Valley'; in Norfolk we say, 'this is like Rhode Island.' The same is true of tourists to the past; one of our chief delights has been to discover the people of the eighteenth century behaving beneath their pomatum and courtliness like people of the twentieth century and to realize that the climate of eighteenth-century opinion is one in which we can, in spite of inclemencies, exist.

There is, for example, the occasion which Horace Walpole describes. He had played late at loo at Lady Jane Scott's and came downstairs to leave with the Duchesses of Grafton and Bedford. He was on very good terms with the Duchess of Grafton who was gay, young, beautiful, and gallant; his relations with the middle-aged Duchess of Bedford were slightly rumpled at the moment. The trio reached the front door to discover that Walpole's chair was not there. He said he would walk until he met a hackney-chair, an eighteenth-century equivalent of a taxi. The Duchess of Grafton, knowing the embarrassment she would cause, said to him that the Duchess of Bedford would take him home. 'There were we charmingly awkward and complimenting,' says Walpole.

'However, she [the Duchess of Bedford] was forced to press it, and I to accept it—in a minute she spied an hackney-chair—"Oh! there is a chair,—but I beg your pardon, it looks as if I wanted to get rid of you, but indeed I don't—only I'm afraid the Duke will want his supper." You may imagine,' Walpole concludes, 'how much I was afraid of making him wait.'[1] This story makes us feel even closer to eighteenth-century London than does the sight of St Paul's rising in the distance. It is the nearest thing to the uninvented machine I spoke of at the beginning of our first tour, the one where you will turn a crank and stir the prints and pictures of the eighteenth century into life.

We of 1941 understand the point of this little story, in spite of the ladies being eighteenth-century duchesses, but the men and women of 1841, as represented by Macaulay, let us say, and Carlyle and Emerson, would have regarded it with contempt. The laughter that it might arouse was particularly objectionable to Carlyle. 'I know that laughter somewhat . . .' he wrote, 'sadder exercise the human muscles cannot well be put to. Spirit, joy, is not in it, only polished malice.'[2] Carlyle spanks us for liking Walpole's story and forces us to remember the training of our youth, the doctrine that life is real, life is earnest, and that there should be no place in it for frivolity.

1. Walpole to Montagu, 26 April 1759.

2. From an unpublished review of Jesse's *George Selwyn and His Contemporaries*, 1843, in the author's possession.

The one theory about history which everyone quotes is that it repeats itself. Although it is rash to do so, one can bracket the three years of our tours with three years in our own lifetime: 1748 and 1920, 1776 and 1930, 1797 and 1940. The analogies cannot be pressed too far, but they exist. In 1920 we were emerging from a war, just as 1748 was. There came with our European experience an awareness of our own past, and the resultant patriotism which showed itself in the rage for collecting American antiques, in the building of 'colonial' houses, and in the employment of genealogists. In 1748 England began taking a more active interest in its own past and history, the most spectacular evidence of which was perhaps the building by Horace Walpole of his toy castle at Strawberry Hill in what he believed to be the true English Gothic spirit. In both years the problem of excessive drinking was in the minds of troubled citizens and in the handling of this problem England of 1748 proved wiser than America of 1920. There is a parallel between the administration of President Harding and the ministries of the Pelhams, in their smugness and corruption. In 1930 we were still displaying opulence and extravagance, although somewhat chastened, as was 1776, by the shocks of the preceding year: Wall Street, like the City, was ineffective in politics. Science was making rapid strides; native talents in the arts were increasingly rewarded. In 1940, as in 1797, a revolution had broken out abroad which we were watching with deepening concern, dimly aware that its effects would alter our own way of living and that the seeds of revolution were present, and might sprout, in our own land. In 1797 England was again at war and her allies had been beaten. More alarming were the divisions at home, the challenge to the old way of life by radicals in the arts and letters, as well as in politics. Blake, Coleridge, and Tom Paine: Picasso, Gertrude Stein, and Franklin Roosevelt. Seventeen hundred and ninety-seven was at the crest of the seventh wave which periodically lifts society and plunges it forward.

The model tourist 'reads up' on the places he is going to visit before he sets out, and before each of our tours we, as model tourists, have done the same. In 1748 we pored over the prints of Hogarth and read the novels of Fielding and Smollett; in 1776 we read Boswell and Walpole. Now in 1797 we depart from our high scholarly standard of consulting only original sources and read a summary of the times written a hundred years later by Sir Walter Besant:

'The eighteenth century prepared itself slowly and unconsciously for the events of its last decade; scholars, historians, and philosophers considered and discussed continually the questions of constitution, government, rights, and liberties. Its travellers wandered over the whole of Europe and elsewhere, observing and reporting on the condition of the people. Everywhere they found kings whose rule was absolute: everywhere they found intolerance in religion; prohibition of free thought; a press muzzled and fettered; judges subservient and corrupt; privileged classes who paid no taxes; the people ground down by exactions, without a voice in the government, without representatives. When they published, or narrated, these things at home, the examination of their own institutions, if only by comparison, was inevitable. They found in this, the boasted land of liberty, a king always trying to filch something more for his prerogative: whose stupid obstinacy in taxing people without representatives had lost England's most magnificent possessions; a civil list blackened by crowds of pensioned favourites; not a tenth part of the people represented; intolerance of free thought; the common people rough and ignorant to the last degree; the army and navy maintained by a barbarous system of flogging which had no parallel even in the Middle Ages; merchants enriched by a trade in slaves far more extensive and more cruel than that formerly carried on by the Saxons; the press rigorously watched; free expression called blasphemy; Catholics, Dissenters, and Jews still under disabilities; a penal code so terrible that juries refused to convict, even with the clearest evidence; and a House of Commons which was the mere tool—the paid, purchased, ignoble tool—of the Government. Worse still, this despicable body prided themselves on being gentlemen and affected to despise tradesmen. Was there ever a worse time for England? Looking around him, the English philosopher could not possibly admit that the British Constitution was the best of all possible constitutions. And when the French Revolution began, undertaking the most sweeping reforms, he could not choose but believe that this was a movement rich in promise, full of generous and noble and humane endeavour, and that this movement would serve as an example to his own country. The frightful excesses which followed damped his ardour. Yet there remained some who continued faithful to their first hopes; and even the long war of twenty-three years which followed, when, for a time, the very existence of Great Britain was in danger, when the Conqueror marched north and south and east throughout a prostrate continent, calling all his own—even these things failed to extinguish in these men the ardent love of liberty which had moved their hearts at the outset: moved their hearts to the very depths: moved all that was in them of generosity and nobility.'[3]

We land at Portsmouth on the ninth of May and are immediately plunged into the revolutionary atmosphere. On the previous day the crews of the Royal Navy had mutinied in Portsmouth Harbor; mutiny had already broken out at St Helens, Spithead, and Plymouth. On the ninth, Admiral Colpoys ordered his marines to fire into

3. Sir Walter Besant, *London in the Eighteenth Century*, 1902, pp. 34–5.

a boatload of insurgent sailors and a dozen men were killed. The air is filled with rumours that the Dutch and Spanish Fleets are about to renew an invasion attempt and that the Brest Fleet is about to sail against Ireland, where the acts of English soldiery are deepening the hatred of England and ensuring the perpetuation of a curse still operative in 1941.

A new foreigner has suddenly appeared in the newspapers, the most formidable name in modern history for one hundred and forty years, the name of a man of obscure birth who has risen to power on the tide of revolution and who now seems unconquerable. The headings of 'The History of Europe' in *The Annual Register* for 1797 have a familiar ring in 1941: 'Buonaparte declares War against the Pope. A French Army enters the Papal Dominions. The Papal Troops completely routed. Buonaparte, by Promises and Threats, induces the Romans to submit to the French, without the Effusion of Blood. Takes Possession of several Provinces in the Ecclesiastical States. Advances towards Rome. Treaty of Peace with the Pope.'[4]

The mutiny of the Fleet brings England to one of the darkest moments in her history. The crews are collected from the riff-raff of society, but their grievances are serious. In the Seven Years War for every man who was killed in action eighty-eight died of disease.[5] The pay of the men has not

4. *The Annual Register*, 1797, p. 1.

5. The figures given in *The Annual Register*, and quoted by Admiral Sir Herbert Richmond in *Johnson's England*, i. 53, are 1,512 killed, 'while 133,708 died of disease or were "missing."'

been increased since the reign of Charles II, in spite of the enormous rise in the cost of living and increases of pay in the army and militia. The distribution of prize money is unfair; the food is shocking; Captain Bligh is representative of the brutality of the officers. The mutinies are to spread to the Nore at the mouth of the Thames during our visit; red flags are to fly at the masts of most of the ships of the Royal Navy until the ringleader of the mutineers is arrested on June 14th and promptly hanged, for he alone will refuse to run down his ship's red flag on the King's birthday, the 4th of June. The picture of the other mutineers doing so reminds us of the pirates of Penzance of a later reign who yielded to Queen Victoria's name.

We leave Portsmouth as rapidly as possible for London which we reach after a night at Guildford. This route takes us across Putney Heath and Westminster Bridge. Horace Walpole, or Lord Orford, as he had become, died in March, but through the kindness of his executrix, Mrs Damer, we are to stay in his house in Berkeley Square, whither he had moved shortly after our last tour. Partly because of the play, Berkeley Square has a special significance for the twentieth century, and though our staying in it is solely due to Walpole's having bought a house there, our arrival in the eighteenth century this year is heightened by the magic of the name.

Berkeley Square is quiet in 1797. Carriages may

roll around either side of it without regard to the direction of the traffic. Several years ago Walpole's royal friend, the Princess Amelia, put up an equestrian statue in the center of the square to her nephew, George III, when he was a promising young man. She had him dressed 'in a Roman habit, in the character of Marcus Aurelius,'[6] which has proved not to be his character at all. Since we were last here shrubs and plane trees have been planted about him. Straw is laid before the houses where a member of the family lies ill; that family is then said to be 'in the straw.' It is all very peaceful.

London has grown still more to the north and south since 1776, and although its growth seems great to the eighteenth century, at most the blocks have extended northwards two-thirds of a mile along a front of a mile and a quarter,[7] which we are bound to consider a modest expansion in half a century. Houses have crossed Oxford Street and reached The New Road, better known to us as the Euston Road, and Portman and Manchester Squares have been built. 'The town is so extended,' Walpole wrote to Miss Berry six years ago, 'the breed of chairs is almost lost, for Hercules and Atlas could not carry anybody from one end of this enormous capital to the other.'[8] The pedestrian gains by this, for the chairs were car-

6. Henry B. Wheatley, *London Past and Present,* 1891, i. 165.
7. Cf. Wallis' map, 1797, with Roque's, 1746.
8. 15 April 1791.

ried rapidly along the footways, and if he did not respond promptly to the chairman's 'By your leave, Sir,' he was in danger of being knocked down.[9]

London is cleaner, brighter and more elegant, to use a favourite word of the time. A new breed of public servants has appeared, the crossing sweepers, who sweep away the dirt before us as we gingerly pick our way across the street.[10] For this they receive half-pence and the charge is not cut for the women sweepers. Their existence means even more tipping, but as the sweeps always take the same corners, another friendly human association has been introduced to London life. The work of erasing London's past continues rapidly. Surviving Elizabethan houses are being demolished with a thoroughness that makes us groan; in their places, we must admit, however, are going up excellent buildings which we are startled to discover are as 'functional' as the 'modern' buildings of the 1930's. The window tax has been increased with deplorable results and is about to be extended still further to include houses with six windows.[11] Still, the houses in the West End are now kept in better condition, thanks to the repairing leases which contain a clause for painting the fronts triannually in an effort to keep the

9. César de Saussure, *A Foreign View of England in the Reigns of George I and George II*, 1902, p. 168.

10. James Peller Malcolm, *Anecdotes of the Manners and Customs of London during the Eighteenth Century*, 1810, ii. 401.

11. See George, *London Life*, p. 77.

'Ancient Inconvenience Contrasted with Modern Convenience. Erected about 1800'

woodwork 'as clean and bright as fogs and coal smoke will permit.'[12]

The struggle with London's dirt and coal smoke has been notable throughout our tours. Women leave their pattens on a high ring beside the front door,[13] and door scrapes are a part of every decent house. The brass knockers, street doors, and locks are scoured and rubbed regularly.[14] Cleanliness is carried to the inside of the house where the French exclaim at the mats and carpets everywhere and the almost daily washing of floors. The young Duc de la Rochefoucauld, however, who was something of a scientist, pursued his researches to the kitchen, a visit he described 'as the worst thing that could befall you . . . before dinner. . . . You may go into the kitchen in a great nobleman's house and see perhaps ten women at work, but I will wager that you will not see a couple of napkins or dish-cloths, and if you do see one in use, you will have no desire to wipe your hands on it, since it is used for everything.'[15]

Washing, at least superficial washing, has extended by 1797 to the owners of the houses, although few have risen to the luxury of Bedford House where there is running hot and cold water, supplied by the New River Company through pipes of elmwood at the rate of seven pounds sixteen shillings a year. Bedford House has also boasted two water closets since 1758, but they are

12. Malcolm, ibid. ii. 402.
13. Kalm, p. 13.
14. Grosley, i. 72–3.
15. *A Frenchman in England*, p. 43.

generations before their time.[16] Washstands have become a recognized feature of the well-appointed bedroom; superb washstands are being made with mirrors and compartments for soap balls and razors,[17] for the gentlemen are not to yield to the temptation of growing whiskers until the nineteenth century is well advanced. I can recall only two bearded Englishmen of the eighteenth century: the beggar-man who appears over and over again in Reynolds' religious and allegorical pictures and Lord George Gordon who grew a beard when he became a Jew. There are a great many public bath houses now where one may take a cold bath daily at the rate of a guinea a year.[18] From the beginning of the century members of the upper classes have washed their hands, arms, faces, necks, and throats *every* day[19] and been none the

16. Gladys Scott Thomson, *The Russells in Bloomsbury*, 1669–1771, 1940, pp. 349–51.

'One of the conveniences of London is that everyone can have an abundance of water. The big reservoir or cistern near Islington, the York Buildings machinery near the Strand, and that of the Bridge supply every quarter abundantly. In every street there is a large principal pipe made of oak wood, and little leaden pipes are adapted to this principal pipe, and carry water into all the houses. Every private individual may have one or two fountains in his house, according to his means, and pays so much a year for each fountain. Water is not obtainable all day, these fountains giving three hours' water in every twenty-four. The large leaden cisterns are replenished during the time the water does not run into the houses. Companies or societies have undertaken this vast enterprise and reap the profits. Besides the distribution of water by the means of pipes, there are in many streets pumps and wells, where poor people who cannot afford to pay for water can obtain it for nothing' (De Saussure, pp. 155–6, writing of the late seventeen-twenties).

17. Oliver Brackett in *Johnson's England*, ii. 144.

18. Archenholz, ii. 128.

19. De Saussure, p. 205.

worse for it. The replacement of wooden bedsteads by iron ones and the introduction of washable cotton clothes are having a salutary effect in the poorer quarters of the town in discouraging the entertainment of vermin. Under George I only one person in five hundred wore stockings; by 1797 almost no one is without them.[20] London has advanced in cleanliness, whatever young Rochefoucauld may have found in the kitchen, since the days when one laundress accommodated the sixty-three persons in the household of George I.[21]

'The exertions of our fathers,' says Malcolm, 'in the general improvement of houses and streets have left *us* little to do. Pure air . . . now circulates freely through the *new* streets; squares, calculated for ornament, health, and the higher ranks of the community, are judiciously dispersed, and their centres converted into beautiful gardens; the tall houses have a sufficient number of large windows; the areas in front are wide, and handsomely railed with cast iron; lamps on scroll-work are suspended at due distances from each other; and admirable level smooth footways of great breadth protect the passenger from the carts and carriages, separated from him by a curb stone raised several inches above spacious kennels, through which the water from showers passes and descends into large drains, communicating with vast sewers many

20. J. L. Hammond, *Rise of Modern Industry*, 1925, p. 210, quoted in John H. Hutchins, *Jonas Hanway*, 1940, p. 151.
21. Ibid. pp. 113–4.

feet below the level of the street.'[22] This cheerful picture is shaded by Malcolm in following paragraphs where he admits that individuals may and do fall short of the excellence of the laws providing for the performance of acts of cleanliness. There are still those, for example, who fail to clear the mud from the pavements before their doors; there are others, mean persons, of course, who 'empty dirty water mixed with their offals into the gutters, the stench of which is appalling,' and we realize that in the midst of change the old survives.

Nothing contributes more to the altered appearance of the streets than the current mode of dress. The spirit of revolution has entered into clothes. Gone are the huge head-dresses, pads, hoops, and long-waisted stays. The bodice is exceedingly décolleté morning and evening; the skirts are thin; the female form is no longer a secret. On their heads women wear long ostrich feathers. Young men have given up wigs and gone in for shaggy hair; they have 'levelled nobility,' in Walpole's phrase.[23] Powder has been given up in protest against the powder-tax. The three-cornered hats have turned into round hats with wide brims. Swords have entirely disappeared except at Court; the umbrella is no longer the sign of a Frenchman. We are astonished by the number of people who are wearing spectacles.[24]

22. Malcolm, ii. 400.
23. To Miss Berry, 26 May 1791.
24. Carl Philipp Moritz, *Travels in England in* 1782, ed. 1926, p. 20.

Dreſs 1797

In the world of social advancement, the dispensary movement which began in 1769 has been greatly extended since 1776. There are now at least fourteen dispensaries at which the poor may attend for advice and free medicine.[25] 'About 50,000 poor persons are thus supplied with medicine and advice gratis, one-third of whom at least are attended' in their own houses.[26] As a result, the health of London is greatly improved and its population, which was stationary during the first half of the century, has taken a sharp rise.[27] And only last year Jenner discovered vaccination.

There are now, in 1797, eighteen prisons in London.[28] Some improvement has been made in prison conditions, thanks chiefly to one of the great humanitarians of the eighteenth century, John Howard, whose work on prisons appeared just after our last tour. Although the selling of liquor in prisons has been stopped, the tedium of prison life is still alleviated by the smuggler. The Fleet, Kings Bench, Bridewell and Newgate were destroyed by the Gordon Rioters in 1780, but the new buildings are scarcely less subject to jail fever or typhus, than were the old. As early as 1774, when 'An Act for Preserving the Health of

25. George, *London Life*, pp. 50, 337.

26. Feltham, *Picture of London*, 1802, p. 167, quoted by George, *London Life*, p. 337.

27. London's population in 1700 was 674,350; in 1750, 676,250; in 1801, 900,000 (George, ibid. p. 329).

28. Patrick Colquhoun, *A Treatise on the Police of the Metropolis*, 1797, p. 388.

Prisoners in Gaol, and Preventing the Gaol Distemper' was introduced, John Lettsom pointed out that merely scraping and whitewashing the cells once a year, keeping the prisons well ventilated, and washing the prisoners on their discharge, was not enough. He did not realize that lice are the cause of typhus, but he did urge the fumigating, or better still, the burning of the prisoners' clothes. However, as the keepers of the prisons make their living by charges extorted from the prisoners and as any sanitary improvements have to come out of their pockets, nothing was done,[29] and now in 1797 jail fever is still common. Since the hospitals admit patients on only one day of the week after a recommendation has been procured, death frequently intervenes before the transfer can be made from prison to hospital.[30] Despite the activities of enlightened philanthropists, nothing in the eighteenth century remains more ferocious than the criminal laws.

It is comforting to hear the Watch still cried at night, 'Past two o'clock and all's well,' although we wish the watchman would put more emphasis on the hour and less on 'past' and 'o'clock.'[31] We

29. James Johnston Abraham, *Lettsom*, 1933, pp. 246, 254–5.

30. See John Hunter, *Observations on Jail and Hospital Fever*, Medical Transactions of the College of Physicians, 1779, quoted by George, *London Life*, p. 337. This practice was continued until the opening of the House of Recovery in 1802, ibid. p. 52.

31. When Boswell in 1790 was carried to Marylebone Watch House for calling the hour in the streets, he gave as his excuse that he was teaching the Watchmen to transfer their emphasis to the hour. (*Private Papers*, 18.20.)

buy the new edition of Colquhuon's *Treatise on the Police of the Metropolis* which has just appeared at Mr Dilly's in the Poultry and alarm ourselves by reading his 'Estimate of Persons who are supposed to support themselves in and near the Metropolis by pursuits either criminal—illegal—or immoral.' The total is 115,000 persons, or one out of every nine people in London. Half of these are prostitutes; 8,500 are cheats of various kinds, swindlers and gamblers 'who live chiefly by fraudulent transactions in the Lottery;' 8,000 are 'Thieves, Pilferers, and Embezzlers;' 4,000 are 'Receivers of Stolen Goods;' 3,000 are coiners; and 2,500 prey upon the docks and arsenals and enjoy the denominations of 'Lumpers, Scuffle-hunters, Mudlarks, Lightermen, and Riggers;' a mere 2,000 are the conventional 'Professed Thieves, Burglars, Highway Robbers, Pick-pockets, and River Pirates.'[32] The laws governing these offences are Draconian: 'There are above one hundred and sixty different offences which subject the parties who are found guilty to the punishment of death without benefit of Clergy,'[33] that is, even though the convicted can write. It is revealing, however, of the public attitude towards these laws that in 1795 only 61 were capitally convicted and only 19 were executed.[34]

How far the humanitarian impulse has yet to

32. Colquhoun, op. cit. pp. vii–xi.
33. Ibid. p. 5.
34. Ibid. p. 230.

move is shown by the continued existence of the chimney-sweeps, who are peculiar to England. They came into being early in the eighteenth century when chimneys began to be narrower as coal supplanted wood and more rooms were attached to a single chimney by complicated flues. The chimney-sweeps are, as a rule, paupers or are sold by their parents for two or three guineas, the smaller the child the better the price. Occasionally they are kidnapped. The average age of the novitiates is about six. Their terror of the black and suffocating ascent may be overcome by their masters lighting straw fires beneath them or by sticking pins into their feet. Since the passages in the chimneys are often only seven inches square, even the tiniest children must be stripped naked before going up. In the beginning they undergo months of suffering until the sores which form on their elbows and knees become cartilaginous. The best masters wash their boys once a week, but most are never washed at all. Many are suffocated or burnt to death; many others become deformed from climbing when their bones are soft.[35]

35. See J. L. Hammond and Barbara Hammond, *The Town Labourer, 1760–1832*, 1936, pp. 176–192, which are largely based on *Commons Reports* and *Journals*, for the statements in this paragraph. 'The last Hertford climbing boy died at Hertford on May 13, 1940, in the person of Daniel Dye, chimney-sweep, aged ninety-three. Members of his family had carried on the business for a century or more; and he was only eight years old when he began working with his father. He told an interviewer, "I did not look forward to it, as one of my brothers had been suffocated to death when climbing up the inside of a chimney, but it was the general thing for the son of a sweep to do." ' (H. C. Andrews in *Notes and Queries*, 22 Feb. 1941, p. 139.)

A marked change since 1776 is the attitude of the people and the press to America. At the time of our first tour an account of what was to become the United States of America was being prepared for a work called *A Museum for Young Gentlemen and Ladies: or, a Private Tutor for little Masters and Misses.*[36] The quality of instruction in this work may be judged by its statement that among the 'commodities' to be found in 'southern Canada' are leopards in Carolina and monkeys in New Jersey.[37] In 1797, on the other hand, the American news in the periodicals and newspapers is reported faithfully and with dignity. We read in *The Gentleman's Magazine*,[38] for example, of the death 'at Norwich, in Connecticut, N. America [of] the Rev. Samuel Seabury, D.D., bishop of that state; one of the most learned and ingenious prelates of the Protestant Episcopal Church in the United States.' In the same magazine under 'American News. Philadelphia, Feb. 8,' we read a careful report of the election of Mr John Adams as President with 71 votes and the election of Mr Thomas Jefferson to the Vice-Presidency with 68 votes, and how Mr Adams, as President of the Senate, read the certificates of the election of the electors from each state, beginning with Tennessee.[39]

The typographical style in which these an-

36. Anon. Printed for J. Hodges and J. Newbery [1750].
37. Ibid. p. 119.
38. 1797, Pt I, pp. 442–3.
39. Ibid. p. 428.

nouncements are made has changed in the fifty years which have passed between them: the substantives no longer appear in capitals, the place-names are no longer in italic. In a year or two the long 's' is to disappear. Benjamin Franklin saw these typographical changes coming and deplored them.[40] The books of 1797 are smaller in size than those of 1748. When Boswell talked of printing his *Life of Johnson* in folio in 1791, Malone told him he 'might as well throw it into the Thames, for a folio would not now be read.'[41] The printing types in vogue are lighter. There is no English printer in 1797 who is producing as brilliant books as the Baskervilles of the 'sixties and 'seventies, but Baskerville's influence upon younger men, together with that of Didot and Bodoni abroad, has been so strong that it has finally reached the great Caslons themselves, and in Mr Updike's phrase, 'Thus the taste for lighter book-printing was carrying all before it by 1800.'[42]

Looking back from 1797 to 1748 we are aware of a change in what was called 'the position of women.' It would be hard to imagine, for example, a man in 1797 locking up his daughter-in-law because of her disinclination to perpetuate his family, and yet we remember this is what Lord Leicester did to Lady Mary Coke in 1748. Fortu-

40. Franklin, *Complete Works*, 1806, ii. 354–6, in a letter to Noah Webster, 26 Dec. 1789.

41. Boswell, *Private Papers*, 18.20.

42. Daniel Berkeley Updike, *Printing Types*, Cambridge, Mass., 1922, ii. 121.

nate women still have a monetary value which is as well known as their names: 'A fortune of six thousand a year;' 'an heiress with thirty thousand in the funds;' but this information is retailed far into the nineteenth century: it is one of the first things Trollope tells us about his characters. In this women have achieved parity with men. In *Pride and Prejudice*, which was completed in this year, we read that Mr Bingley's friend, 'Mr Darcy, soon drew the attention of the room by his fine, tall person, handsome features, noble mien, and the report, which was in general circulation within five minutes after his entrance, of his having ten thousand a year.'

Although by twentieth-century standards woman's advancement in the eighteenth century was modest, it was, nevertheless, steady. By comparison with the salons of Mme du Deffand and Mlle de Lespinasse the Conversation Parties of Mrs Montagu and the rest were rather ridiculous, but women did venture forth not only into the arena of polite conversation but into fields hitherto held to be exclusively male. Mrs Elizabeth Carter translated Epictetus and was mistress of no less than eight languages; Miss Berry commanded almost as many;[42a] Fanny Burney was the leading novelist of her time and was followed by Jane Austen, and during their supremacy the vogue of

42a. Chesterfield in 1750 observed that Lady Hervey understood Latin 'though she wisely conceals it' (letter to his son, 22 Oct. 1750 O.S.). Mrs Carter and Miss Berry did not conceal their learning.

the Gothic novel was maintained by Clara Reeve and Mrs Radcliffe. Hannah More, after establishing herself as a playwright, became a major influence with her 'Cheap Repository Tracts,' which were written to make people 'good'; Angelica Kauffmann was one of the original members of the Royal Academy; Mrs Damer achieved an international reputation as a sculptress; Mrs Catherine Macaulay attained the same as an historian and a controversialist and acquired the remarkable distinction of moving both Wilkes and Dr Johnson to unmannerly remarks upon her use of cosmetics;[43] Mary Wollstonecraft, the passionate follower of Rousseau, sounded a new note with her *Vindication of the Rights of Woman*, the phrase which was to become a battle-cry over a century later. Edmund Burke said that the most notable feature of his age was the number of extraordinary women it had produced.

There has been since 1748 a diminution in the exactions of servants. At that time when one left a private house after a meal the five or six footmen in it lined up in the hall, and if one did not give them each a shilling he regretted it on his next appearance at the house.[44] If the footmen were in livery, one had to give them half a crown.[45] These

43. 'Johnson said it was better that she should "redden her own cheeks" than "blacken other people's characters,"' and 'Wilkes ... described her as "painted up to the eyes" and looking "as rotten as an old withered pear."' (DNB, *sub* Catherine Macaulay.)

44. De Saussure, p. 194. Grosley says that this practice was given over by 1765, i. 76.

45. Count Frederick Kielmansegge, *Diary of a Journey to England in the Years* 1761–1762, 1902, pp. 53–4.

tips were called 'vales.' In addition to them, one was expected to give Christmas boxes to the servants of one's friends.[46] Now in 1797 the wages of servants have been raised: a scrubbing maid may get seven guineas a year and a guinea for her tea; a cook gets all of twenty guineas. Unlike the footmen they may have to supply their own clothes, which they try to have as fine as their mistress', an ambition frequently achieved by the simple expedient of appropriating her clothes in her absence. The insolence and rapacity of the men servants in their fine liveries are still remarkable. A negro servant, like Dr Johnson's Frank Barber, may still be found in the houses of the great, although Wilberforce is moving heaven and earth to abolish the slave trade. Servants remain throughout the eighteenth century a problem for its housekeepers.

The two generations of our tours have also seen a change in the treatment of upper-class children in the direction of leniency. Earlier in the century children knelt for their parents' blessing on getting up and going to bed, and when they had received it, they kissed their parents' hands.[47] Now in 1797 Mr Bennet (of *Pride and Prejudice*) permits his younger daughters to run after the officers, even though he sees that they are making fools of themselves, but youth is not yet a cult; its physical superiority and good looks are not yet a mecca to

46. De Saussure, p. 195, says that Sir Robert Walpole's porter received nearly £80 at Christmas.

47. Ibid., p. 296.

be struggled for as advancing years draw one relentlessly farther from it. The generations mingle more easily now than they do in twentieth-century America, where, for some reason, we are more self-conscious about our ages. Sheridan wrote *The Rivals* when he was twenty-four; at the same age the younger Pitt was Prime Minister and his great rival, Charles Fox, was a national figure. At twenty-three Boswell became acquainted with Johnson. Years, or the lack of them, are not particularly important in the eighteenth century.

Few of the older figures we associate with the eighteenth century are to survive 1797. Besides Walpole, Burke, Wilkes, and William Mason die in this year. On the death of Mason, Miss Anna Seward, 'The Swan of Litchfield,' a formidable poetess and critic, re-read his *English Garden* and wept so luxuriously that her tears were 'yet wet' on her cheeks even after writing her correspondent at some length.[48] Mason's rank as a lyric poet, she declares, 'is but one degree below Gray who was unquestionably the first lyric poet the world has produced.'[49] She has found many lines to admire in *The Vales of Wever* just published by John Gisborne, 'The Man of Prayer,' and records in her copy[50] opposite the lines

And as they chas'd the breeze of night,
Their blue eyes sparkled with delight

the single, definitive word, 'sweet.' While Miss

48. *Letters of Anna Seward*, Edinburgh, 1811, iv. 365.
49. Ibid. iv. 364.
50. Now in the writer's possession.

Seward was thus employed, Wordsworth and Coleridge were completing their manuscript of *The Lyrical Ballads*.

Seventeen hundred and ninety-seven is a revolutionary year, but the Old Order is not inarticulate and it has enlisted the support of some of the most brilliant younger men in England. One of these is George Canning, who in 1797 is twenty-seven. On coming down from Oxford he was introduced to Devonshire House, the great Whig stronghold, by Fox and Sheridan, but the French Revolution made him a Tory, as it did Burke and Walpole and many others. Sir Walter Scott says that his conversion was due to a visit from William Godwin who told Canning that in the event of a revolution the English Jacobins had determined to make him their leader. In November 1797 appeared the following lines by Canning in the *Anti-Jacobin*. I quote them in full to show how, for once, a conservative met the revolutionary spirit with wit and skill and how the ruling classes now condescend to oppose republican principles. England did not go the way of France and these lines perhaps show us why. They are called 'The Friend of Humanity and the Knife-Grinder.'

THE FRIEND OF HUMANITY AND THE KNIFE-GRINDER

FRIEND OF HUMANITY

'*Needy Knife-grinder! whither are you going?*
Rough is the road, your Wheel is out of order—
Bleak blows the blast;—your hat has got a hole in't,
So have your breeches!

'Weary Knife-grinder! little think the proud ones,
Who in their coaches roll along the turnpike—
—road, what hard work 'tis crying all day "Knives and
Scissors to grind O!"

'Tell me, Knife-grinder, how you came to grind knives?
Did some rich man tyranically use you?
Was it the 'Squire? or Parson of the Parish?
Or the Attorney?

'Was it the 'Squire for killing of his Game? or
Covetous Parson for his Tythes distraining?
Or roguish Lawyer made you lose your little
All in a law-suit?

'(*Have you not read* The Rights of Man, *by Tom Paine?*)
Drops of compassion tremble on my eye-lids,
Ready to fall, as soon as you have told your
Pitiful story.'

KNIFE-GRINDER

'Story! God bless you! I have none to tell, Sir,
Only last night a-drinking at the Chequers,
This poor old hat and breeches, as you see, were
Torn in a scuffle.

'Constables came up for to take me into
Custody; they took me before the Justice;
Justice Oldmixon put me in the Parish—
—Stocks for a Vagrant.

'I should be glad to drink your Honour's health in
A Pot of Beer, if you would give me Sixpence;
But for my part; I never love to meddle
With Politics, Sir.'

FRIEND OF HUMANITY

'I *give thee Sixpence! I will see thee damn'd first—*
Wretch! whom no sense of wrongs can rouse to vengeance—
Sordid, unfeeling, reprobate, degraded,
Spiritless outcast!'[50a]

50a. *The Anti-Jacobin*, No. 2, 27 Nov. 1797.

The Royal Academy exhibition has just opened with six pictures by the new President, Benjamin West, portraits of Kemble and Mrs Siddons by Lawrence who also contributes 'Satan Calling Up the Fallen Angels from the Fiery Lake,' in which the 'figure of Satan,' according to *The Times*, 'is at least twelve feet high.'[51] Hoppner is represented by 'Mrs Sheridan with her child at her back, in the character of a gypsy,' and four others. Among the drawings are Wyatt's 'of a Gothic building for Mr Beckford's seat at Fonthill,' and another design 'of a Gothic mausoleum for the Grosvenor family, as seen by moonlight.'[52]

James Wyatt is the first of the modern 'Gothic' architects, the forerunner of Pugin and the deluge. He put the finishing touches to Strawberry Hill in 1790, and so was in the apostolic succession. His contribution to Strawberry was in what Walpole called 'the collegiate style,' as opposed to the 'cathedral and castle styles,'[53] in which the earlier rooms were built. Wyatt is the professional Goth who has taken up the work of gifted amateurs and given it legitimate standing, a standing not impaired when his Gothic building for Mr Beckford's seat at Fonthill fell down.

In our last tour I spoke of the new sights of London, the British Museum and the Royal

51. 29 April.
52. Loc. cit.
53. So styled by Walpole in a MS note in his copy of Archibald Robertson, *A Topographical Survey of the Great Road from London to Bath and Bristol*, 1792, i. 34, now in the British Museum.

Academy Exhibition. There was a third sight then to which every foreigner of distinction repaired, Strawberry Hill, which was only ten miles from Hyde Park Corner, and now, although its creator is no longer living, Mrs Damer has arranged for us to visit it once more.

The first impression Strawberry Hill makes on us is of its smallness; it really is a toy castle set in an enamelled lawn; and the second impression is of its attractiveness, of which the prints give no hint. Walpole played an important part in the eighteenth-century revolt from the formal garden and the development of the English garden with its dedication to the appearance of simplicity. Trees were permitted to grow as nature willed without the interference of the topiary artist; borders were planted, and the lawn, the feature of a garden which appears the most natural and is actually the most artificial, was carefully rolled and cut. The trees and borders and lawns at Strawberry are a delight.

The house itself is curiously pleasing for one which has been held up to such ridicule. It is crenellated and has pointed windows and a few pinnacles are nailed on here and there with an effect of old-fashioned scenery, but these romantic flourishes are only a thin disguise beneath which the Georgian frame is plainly visible. At the end of his life, Walpole admitted that Wyatt had shown the 'imperfections and bad execution of my attempts,' for, Walpole confessed, he and his collaborators in the house had not studied 'the

Strawberry Hill, South Front

science.'[54] 'Every true Goth must perceive that [the rooms] are more the works of fancy than of imitation,' he wrote.[54a] But when the rooms were planned Walpole believed that he was proceeding on scientific lines. He picked out details which he liked of authentic Gothic buildings and incorporated them into the house: the ceiling of Henry the Seventh's Chapel at Westminster covered his Gallery; the tomb of Archbishop Warham in Canterbury was boiled down into a chimney-piece in a bedroom; the side doors to the choir of Old St Paul's shrank to frames which swung on hinges before the bookshelves in the Library and gave the appearance of the ancient while preserving the convenience of the modern. Those Gothic frames swinging solemnly on their hinges before the plain, everyday, shelves epitomize Strawberry Hill. The eighteenth century finds nothing absurd in 'imitating' Gothic details in modern houses, nothing incongruous in translating sepulchral monuments into chimney-pieces, and nothing ostentatious in sticking into the windows panes of glass painted with the arms of ancestors recently exhumed to prove that one was, despite new money, of ancient race. The word 'snob' has not yet been invented; the eighteenth century has found Strawberry Hill what its master intended it to be, a romantic escape. 'Visions, you know,' Walpole wrote,[55] 'have always been my pasture. . . . I almost think

54. Walpole to Barrett, 5 June 1788.
54a. To Miss Berry, 17 Oct. 1794.
55. To Montagu, 5 Jan. 1766.

there is no wisdom comparable to that of exchanging what is called the realities of life for dreams. Old castles, old pictures, old histories, and the babble of old people, make one live back into centuries, that cannot disappoint one. One holds fast and surely what is past. The dead have exhausted their power of deceiving—one can trust Catherine of Medicis now.'

Walpole and his collaborators knew nothing of stresses and strains, but they fortunately had the services of a builder who could put up a house so that it would not fall down. Strawberry Hill is largely lath and plaster, and it was said[55a] long before Walpole died that he had already outlived three sets of his battlements, but Strawberry Hill still stands in 1941. There is a Strawberry Hill post-office and telegraph office in 1941; one can buy a railway ticket to Strawberry Hill. London has reached out and encircled it, two-family villas shut off its views of the Thames, but the flimsy building has survived all assaults, including those of the bombers who only the other night destroyed its nearest neighbours.

Strawberry Hill was a show place in the eighteenth century, visited by the famous from all over Europe as well as from Britain. 'Strawberry ... has been more sumptuous today than ordinary, and banqueted their representative majesties of

55a. By 'Gilly' Williams; see Horace Walpole, *Correspondence with Mme du Deffand*, Yale edn, ii. 251, n. 19.

France and Spain. I had Monsieur and Madame de Guerchy, Mademoiselle de Nangis their daughter, two other French gentlemen, the Prince of Masserano, his brother and secretary, Lord March, George Selwyn, Mrs Anne Pitt, and my niece Waldegrave. The refectory never was so crowded: nor have any foreigners been here before that comprehended Strawberry. Indeed everything succeeded to a hair. A violent shower in the morning laid the dust, brightened the green, refreshed the roses, pinks, orange-flowers, and the blossoms with which the acacias are covered. A rich storm of thunder and lightning gave a dignity of colouring to the heavens, and the sun appeared enough to illuminate the landscape, without basking himself over it at his length. During dinner, there were French horns and clarinets in the cloister, and after coffee I treated them with an English and to them very new collation, a syllabub, milked under the cows that were brought to the brow of the terrace. Thence they went to the printing-house, and saw a new fashionable French song printed. They drank tea in the gallery, and at eight went away to Vauxhall!'[56] Strawberry was perfectly unique. There were those who made fun of it, as did Beckford who called it a 'Gothic mouse-trap,' and Walpole's neighbour, Miss Lætitia-Matilda Hawkins, was speaking for many when she referred to it as Walpole's 'bauble-villa'

56. Walpole to Montagu, 18 June 1764.

and a 'crazy bargain,'[56a] but the *cognoscenti* took it seriously; they 'comprehended' Strawberry.

Entering by the north gate now in 1797, in the spirit of make-believe which Walpole asked of his visitors, we are forced to admit that he has, in part, at least, succeeded. The Little Gallery, for all its tininess, does suggest the fourteenth century, the façade of the north entrance, with its row of ancestral shields does announce a feudal dwelling, the narrow saints in the windows by the door do cast a rich and mysterious gloom. Once inside we wander through the little rooms with rapidly mounting 'museum-fatigue.' No house ever had so much in so little. There are scores of pictures and miniatures and enamels by famous names; there are hundreds of objects of art: snuff-boxes, toothpick cases, rosaries, smelling-boxes, rings, cameos, intaglios, and bronzes. It is to take thirty-two days in 1842 to sell them all off.

In all this welter we pay particular attention to the Library which is disposed in three rooms. It contains about seven thousand volumes in all. This is not a large library by eighteenth-century standards, but Walpole has annotated about a third of it. There are Latin and French classics in the original, a few Italian and Greek classics, as well, and all the English classics, mostly in mod-

56a. Lætitia-Matilda Hawkins, *Anecdotes, Biographical Sketches and Memoirs*, 1822, i. 87. Miss Hawkins also says that Walpole's 'external decorations frequently provoked the wanton malice of the lower classes, who, almost as certainly as new pinnacles were put to a pretty Gothic entrance, broke them off' (loc. cit.).

ern editions. As the author of *A Catalogue of Royal and Noble Authors*, Walpole made a point of collecting their works and he had a particular weakness for topographical books and county histories.[57] His collection of English prints was probably the finest ever made. He bought the contemporary plays, poems and pamphlets as they appeared and bound them up, ten items or so to a volume, with his arms on the sides, and a 'List of Contents' written by him on the inside cover. He annotated these in conscious preparation of the history of his own time and with his mind always on assisting posterity. The creation of such a library is as characteristic of the eighteenth century and as foreign to the twentieth as are pillories and sedan chairs and the ability of men of affairs to write easy occasional verses which are not only witty but which scan as well.[58]

Walpole did not collect the Elizabethan quartos which he might have done with so little competition, and comparatively few books in the library are to bring high prices in the twentieth century. A notable exception is a sixteenth-century psalter illuminated by Julio Clovio for Nicholas of Anjou. Walpole was careful to record the history of his possessions and he took particular pains with the history of this manuscript. 'Such well-attested

57. 'I am sorry I have such predilection for the histories of particular counties and towns,' he wrote, 'there certainly does not exist a worse class of reading.' (Walpole to Cole, 6 March 1780.)

58. The chief sources for any study of Strawberry Hill are Walpole's *Description* of it and the 1842 Sale Catalogue of it.

descent,' he wrote, 'is the genealogy of the objects of virtù—not so noble as those of the peerage, but on a par with those of race-horses. In all three, especially the pedigrees of peers and rarities, the line is often continued by many insignificant names.'[59] The Psalter illuminated by Julio Clovio was acquired early in the seventeenth century by the Second Earl of Arundel and was bought in 1720 at the sale of his collection by Edward Harley, Earl of Oxford, who bequeathed it to his daughter, the Duchess of Portland. It was bought at her sale in 1786 by Horace Walpole for £169.1.0,[60] who has added his bookplate as Earl of Orford. In the Strawberry Hill Sale in 1842 it was bought by Lord Waldegrave for £441. It is now in Providence, at the John Carter Brown Library, and we have here a genealogy which has been uniformly noble.

Already in 1797 Strawberry Hill is a little dated. The Gothic business is being done on a much more elaborate and costly scale at Fonthill and elsewhere. Wyatt's new houses have a ponderousness which is to press out the 'fancy' of Walpole's attempts and to lead ultimately to what in our own country is to be known as 'General Grant Gothic.' To Walpole must go the dubious celebrity of being the progenitor of one of the worst architectural styles in history, but Strawberry itself has the freshness and the sparkle of a spring—or, rather, of an artesian well.

59. Preface to *A Description of Strawberry Hill*, 1784.

60. So stated by Walpole in his catalogue of the sale (now in the writer's possession).

As we walk about the little passages and into these fabulous rooms the eighteenth-century men and women whom we know seem to press about us, together with hundreds more who merely came with their tickets of admission, which were limited to four persons a day. These last were usually shown about by Margaret Young, the housekeeper, while Walpole himself kept out of sight with his dogs and cats and books. Mrs Young is dead now in 1797 and we have been shown about by her successor, Ann Bransom, who has just inherited one hundred pounds from her master. We give her a guinea when we say good-bye at the gate in the wall which runs along the road, and the towers and pinnacles of Strawberry Hill, of the eighteenth century itself, it almost seems, are shut behind us.

A year or two after this our last tour, Col. George Hanger, Lord Coleraine, made two remarkable prophecies about America. The first has been fulfilled: the war between our Northern and Southern states. The second prophecy was even more remarkable and has been partially fulfilled since I began these lectures. 'I anxiously hope and trust I shall live to see the day,' Hanger wrote, 'when an alliance offensive and defensive will be formed between [our] two countries; as Great Britain and America may defy the united powers of Europe.'[61] Colonel Hanger was the friend of the

61. Col. George Hanger, *Life, Adventures, and Opinions*, 1801, pp. 433–4.

Prince Regent and was not an exemplary man. He was not moved by the visions which inspired men in England, France, and America at the end of the eighteenth century to rhapsodies on the perfectability of man and the coming concord of nations. He was a dissolute realist who hoped for a practical alternative to Britain's recurrent wars.

That such a man should have a touch of the mystic should not surprise us after our three tours, for we have found contradictions on every hand. We have seen the coarse and the delicate existing side by side: the London of Hogarth, Rowlandson, and Gillray and the London of Zoffany, Reynolds, and Lawrence. We have seen man's inhumanity to man; we have seen man dedicating himself to the trivial and wasteful; we have seen him aspiring to a nobler state with hope and charity. As for his faith, we may close with the vision of Blake whose God, in Professor Foster Damon's words, 'is a friend who descends and raises man till man himself is a god,'[62] and we may ponder a drawing by Blake to illustrate these lines of Young:

> *Nature revolves but man advances. Both*
> *Eternal: that a circle, this a line.*[63]

Blake's illustration of this is 'a serpent coiled upon itself, endlessly revolving; while above it stands man, a straight line poised upon the circle.'[64]

62. S. Foster Damon, *William Blake: His Philosophy and Symbols*, Boston, 1924, p. x.

63. *Night Thoughts*, vi. 692–3.

64. Damon, op. cit. pp. 140, 345.

BIBLIOGRAPHY

The number of books on London in the eighteenth century is legion. I give here only those which I have cited in the text. Many more are listed at the end of the chapters in *Johnson's England*, a book to which, with Miss George's invaluable *London Life in the XVIII Century*, I am particularly indebted. All the books listed here were published in London unless otherwise stated.

ABRAHAM, JAMES JOHNSTON. *Lettsom, His Life, Times, Friends, and Descendants*, 1933.

ANDREWS, ALEXANDER. *The Eighteenth Century*, 1856.

ANDREWS, H. C. In *Notes and Queries*, 22 Feb. 1941.

Annual Register, The. 1763, 1765, July 4, 1776, 1797.

Anon. *The Conduct of the Four Managers of Covent-Garden Theatre, by a Frequenter of the Theatre*, 1768.

Anon. *The General Shop Book: or, The Tradesman's Universal Director*, 1753.

Anon. *The History of Whites*, 2 vols, n.d. [preface, June 1892].

Anon. *Narrative of the Journey of an Irish Gentleman through England in the Year* 1752, ed. W. C. Hazlitt, 1869.

Anon. *Some Customs Considered Whether Prejudicial to the Health of This City*, 1721.

ARCHENHOLZ, J. W. VON. *A Picture of England*, 2 vols, 1789.

AUSTEN, JANE. *Pride and Prejudice*. (Completed in 1797.)

Baily's Racing Register, from the Earliest Records to the Close of the Year 1842, 3 vols, 1845.

BECKER, CARL. *The Heavenly City of the Eighteenth-Century Philosophers*, New Haven, 1932.

BELLAMY, GEORGE ANNE. *An Apology for the Life of George Anne Bellamy, late of Covent Garden Theatre, Written by Herself*, 6 vols, 1785.

BESANT, SIR WALTER. *London in the Eighteenth Century*, 1902.

BLEACKLEY, HORACE. *Casanova in England* [1923].

BOSWELL, JAMES. *The Life of Samuel Johnson, LL.D.*, ed. George Birkbeck Hill and L. F. Powell, 6 vols, 1934.

BOSWELL, JAMES. *Private Papers of James Boswell from Malahide Castle*, ed. Geoffrey Scott and Frederick A. Pottle, privately printed, 18 vols, 1928–1934.

BURNEY, FRANCES. *Evelina; or, The History of a Young Lady's Entrance into the World*. (First published 1778), edn 1920.

CAMPBELL, R. *The London Tradesman*, 1747.

CAMPBELL, THOMAS. *Life of Mrs Siddons*, 2 vols, 1834.

CANNING, GEORGE. *The Friend of Humanity and the Knife-Grinder. The Anti-Jacobin*, No. 2, November 27, 1797—reprinted in *The Oxford Book of Eighteenth Century Verse*, 1926.

CARLYLE, THOMAS. Unpublished review of J. H. Jesse's *George Selwyn and His Contemporaries*, 1843, in the possession of W. S. Lewis.

A Catalogue of the Superb Household Furniture . . . of The Hon. Mr Damer, *dec. at His Late Mansion in Tilney Street, May Fair . . . which will be sold by Auction on the Premises . . . February the 3d*, 1777, *and the nine following days.*

A Catalogue of the Portland Museum, Lately the Property of The Duchess Dowager of Portland: Which will be sold by Auction, by Mr Skinner and Co. on Monday the 24th of April, 1786, *and the Thirty-Seven Following Days.*

CHAMBERLAYNE, JOHN. *Magnae Britanniæ Notitia: or, The Present State of Great Britain*, 1755.

COKE, LADY MARY. Unpublished journals in the possession of the Earl of Home, K.T.

COLQUHOUN, PATRICK. *A Treatise on the Police of the Metropolis*, 1797.

Commons Journals, 13 March 1776, vol. 35, and vol. 29, 1762.

The Connoisseur, 31 January 1754.

CRANE, RONALD S. and KAYE, FRED B. *A Census of British Newspapers and Periodicals*, 1620–1800, Chapel Hill, 1927.

CURWEN, SAMUEL. *Journal and Letters of Samuel Curwen*, ed. George Atkinson Ward, New York, 1845.

The Daily Advertiser, 2 July and 24 August 1748.

DAMON, S. FOSTER. *William Blake: His Philosophy and Symbols*, Boston, 1924.

DEFOE, DANIEL. *Review*, 9 May 1713. (Reprinted for the Facsimile Text Society, N.Y., 1938.)

Dictionary of National Biography, sub Sir John Fielding and Catherine Macaulay.

DUNLAP, WILLIAM. *A History of the Rise and Progress of the Arts of Design in the United States*, 3 vols, Boston, 1918.

FELTHAM, JOHN. *The Picture of London for* 1802.

FIELDING, HENRY. *An Enquiry into the Causes of the late Increase of Robbers*, 1751.

FRANKLIN, BENJAMIN. *Complete Works*, 3 vols, 1806.

GARRICK, DAVID. *An Essay on Acting*, 1744.
The General Contents of the British Museum, 1761.
The Gentleman's Magazine, 1748, 1749, 1774, 1776, 1789, 1797.
GEORGE, M. DOROTHY. *London Life in the XVIII Century*, 1925.
GISBORNE, JOHN. *The Vales of Wever*, 1797.
GRAVES, ALGERNON. *The Royal Academy of Arts. A Complete Dictionary of Contributors*, 8 vols, 1905–1906.
GROSLEY, PETER J. *A Tour to London; or, New Observations on England and Its Inhabitants*, trans. Thomas Nugent, 2 vols, 1772.
HAMMOND, J. L. *Rise of Modern Industry*, 1925.
HAMMOND, J. L. and BARBARA. *The Town Labourer*, 1760–1832 [1936].
HAMPDEN, JOHN. *An Eighteenth-Century Journal, Being a Record of the Years* 1774–1776, 1940.
HANGER, COL. GEORGE. *The Life, Adventures, and Opinions of Col. George Hanger*, 2 vols, 1801.
HARRISON, MRS SARAH (of Devonshire). *The House-keeper's Pocket Book* [1783].
HAWKINS, MISS LÆTITIA-MATILDA. *Anecdotes, Biographical Sketches and Memoirs*, 3 vols, 1822.
HOME, GORDON. *Old London Bridge*, 1931.
HUME, DAVID. *The Letters of David Hume*, ed. J. Y. T. Greig, 2 vols, Oxford, 1932.
HUNTER, JOHN, M.D. *Observations on the Disease Commonly Called the Jail or Hospital Fever*, 'Medical Transactions of the College of Physicians,' (1779).
HUTCHINS, JOHN H. *Jonas Hanway*, 1940.
JACKMAN, W[ILLIAM] T. *The Development of Transportation in Modern England*, 2 vols, Cambridge, 1916.
Johnson's England, 2 vols, ed. A. S. Turberville, 1933.
Sir Frank Mackinnon. 'The Law and the Lawyers.'
Sir D'Arcy Power. 'Medicine.'
Admiral Sir Herbert Richmond. 'The Navy.'
Oliver Brackett. 'The Interior of the House.'
M. Dorothy George. 'London and the Life of the Town.'
Johnsonian Miscellanies, ed. George Birkbeck Hill, 2 vols, 1897.
KALM, PEHR. *Kalm's Account of His Visit to England on His Way to America in* 1748, trans. Joseph Lucas, 1892.
KIELMANSEGGE, COUNT FREDERICK. *Diary of a Journey to England in the Years* 1761–1762, 1902.

La Rochefoucauld, François de. *A Frenchman in England*, 1784, *Being the* Mélanges sur l'Angleterre *of François de la Rochefoucauld*, trans. S. C. Roberts, Cambridge, 1933.

Lecky, William E. H. *A History of England in the Eighteenth Century*, 8 vols, 1883–90.

Locke, John. *Civil Government*, 1690.

London Chronicle, 2 June 1764.

Malcolm, James Peller. *Anecdotes of the Manners and Customs of London During the Eighteenth Century*, 2 vols, 1810.

Mandeville, Bernard. *The Fable of the Bees*, 1714.

The Memoirs of Jacques Casanova, ed. Arthur Machen, 12 vols in 6, 1928.

More, Hannah. *Memoirs of the Life and Correspondence of Mrs Hannah More*, ed. William Roberts, 4 vols, 1834.

Moritz, Carl Philipp. *Travels of Carl Philipp Moritz in England in* 1782, edn 1926.

The Morning Post, 4 Sept. 1776, 22 May 1776, 2 October 1776.

A Museum for Young Gentlemen and Ladies: or, A Private Tutor for Little Masters and Misses. Printed for J. Hodges and J. Newbery [1750].

Namier, L[ewis] B. *England in the Age of the American Revolution*, 1930.

Nicoll, Allardyce. *A History of Late Eighteenth Century Drama*, 1750–1800, Cambridge, 1927.

Noorthouck, John. *A New History of London, Including Westminster and Southwark*, 1773.

Notes and Queries, 10th and 11th Series, 1907–12; 22 Feb. 1941.

Odell, George C. D. *Shakespeare from Betterton to Irving*, 2 vols, New York, 1921.

Old England, 2 July 1748, 6 August 1748.

Order Book, Middlesex Sessions, January 1735/6.

Paston, George. *Social Caricature in the Eighteenth Century* [1905].

Peake, Richard Brinsley. *Memoirs of the Colman Family* [1841], 2 vols in 1.

Pennant, Thomas. *Of London*, 1790.

Pritchett, V. S. *The New Statesman and Nation*, 2 Nov. 1940, 'Books in General.'

Private Charity in England, 1747–1757, ed. W. S. Lewis and Ralph M. Williams, New Haven, 1938.

The Public Advertiser, 4 May 1776; 6 Jan. 1777.

Richardson, J. *Recollections*, 1856.

Robertson, Archibald. *A Topographical Survey of the Great Road from London to Bath and Bristol*, 1792.

Rocque, John. *Plan of London*, 1746.

Saint Fond, Barthélemy Faujas de. *A Journey through England and Scotland to the Hebrides in* 1784, ed. Sir Archibald Geikie, Glasgow, 2 vols, 1907.

Saussure, César de. *A Foreign View of England in the Reigns of George I and George II*, trans. and ed. by Madame Van Muyden, 1902.

Seward, Anna. *Letters of Anna Seward*, 6 vols, Edinburgh, 1811.

Smollett, Tobias. *Roderick Random*, 1748.

Stewart, James. *Plocacosmos: or, The Whole Art of Hair Dressing*, 1782.

Strawberry Hill, A Catalogue of the Classic Contents of, 1842.

Thaler, Alwin. *Shakespere to Sheridan, A Book About the Theatre of Yesterday and Today*, Cambridge, Mass., 1922.

Thomson, Gladys Scott. *The Russells in Bloomsbury*, 1669–1771, 1940.

The Times, 29 April 1797.

Tinker, Chauncey Brewster. *Nature's Simple Plan*, Princeton, 1921.

The Town and Country Magazine, 1776.

Updike, Daniel Berkeley. *Printing Types*, 2 vols, Cambridge, Mass., 1922.

Wallis' Plan of the Cities of London and Westminster, 1797.

Walpole, Horace. *Correspondence with Mme du Deffand*, 6 vols, ed. W. S. Lewis and W. H. Smith (Yale edn), New Haven, 1939.

Walpole, Horace. *A Description of Strawberry Hill*, Strawberry Hill, 1784.

Walpole, Horace. *The Last Journals of Horace Walpole During the Reign of George III*, from 1771–83, ed. A. Francis Steuart, 2 vols, 1910.

Walpole, Horace. *Notes by Horace Walpole on Several Characters of Shakespeare*, ed. W. S. Lewis, privately printed, Farmington, Conn., 1940.

Weekly Miscellany, 1 March 1735.

Wesley, John, *The Journal of John Wesley*, ed. Nora Ratcliff, 1940.

Wheatley, Henry B. *London, Past and Present*, 3 vols, 1891.

Wilkinson, Tate. *Memoirs of His Own Life*, 4 vols, York, 1790.

Young, Edward. *The Complaint, and the Consolation; or, Night Thoughts* [with engravings by William Blake], 1797.

INDEX

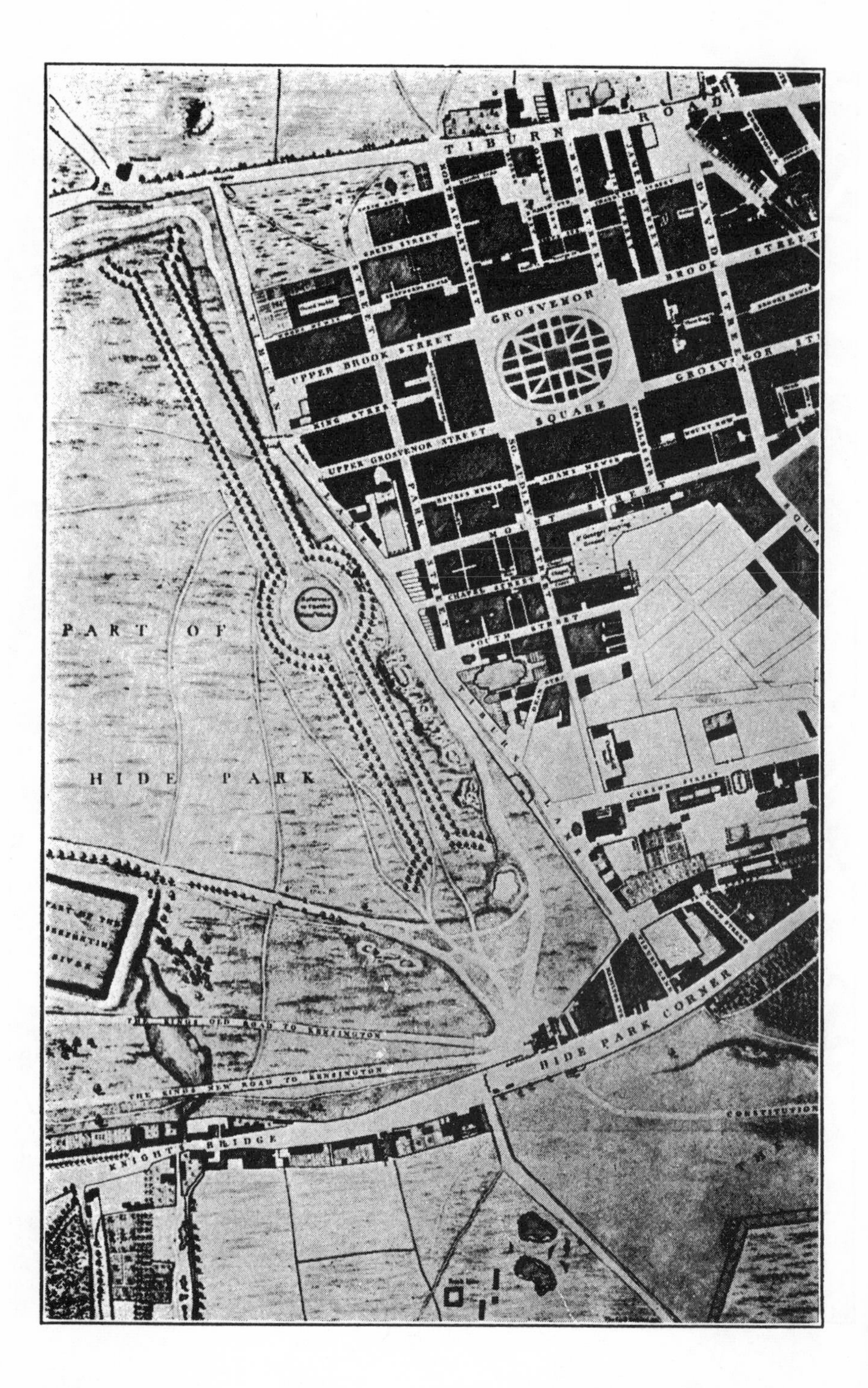

TIBURN ROAD
GROSVENOR SQUARE
BROOK STREET
UPPER BROOK STREET
KING STREET
UPPER GROSVENOR STREET
MOUNT STREET
CHAPEL STREET
SOUTH STREET
CURZON STREET
PART OF
HIDE PARK
HIDE PARK CORNER
KNIGHT BRIDGE
CONSTITUTION

HANOVER SQUARE
PRINCES STR.
HANOVER STREET
GREAT GEORGE STREET
CONDUIT STREET
BOND STREET
BRUTON STREET
BERKELEY STREET
PICCADILLY
DEAN STREET
BROAD STREET
GOLDEN SQUARE
LEICESTER FIELDS
THE HAY MARKET
ST. JAMES'S SQUARE
CHARLES STREET
PALL MALL
ST. JAMES'S STREET
KING STREET
GREEN PARK
ST. JAMES'S PARK

PARLIAMENT STREET
BRIDGE STREET
WESTMINSTER BRIDGE
NEW PALACE YARD
THE NEW ROAD
Timber Yard
Timber Yard

R I V E R
CORNHILL
FENCHURCH
THE BOROUGH